THE Practice OF Love

*The Art of Growing in Greater
Love of Yourself, Others and God*

DAVE BESWICK

AMA Publishing

No portion of this material is intended to offer personal, psychological, spiritual, or professional advice. The information contained herein cannot replace or substitute for the services of trained professionals in any field, including, but not limited to, psychological or spiritual matters. Under no circumstances, will David E. Beswick or Beswick Enterprises or any of its representatives or contractors be liable for any special or consequential damages that result from the use of, or the inability to use, the information or strategies communicated through this material. You alone are responsible or accountable for your decisions, actions and results in life, and by your use of these materials, you agree not to attempt to hold us liable for any such decisions, actions or results, at any time, under any circumstance.

Cover Designer and Formatting:	Amanda Wolfe growcolab.com
Editor:	Marissa Wells

Library of Congress Cataloguing-in-Publication Data

Names:	Beswick, Dave, 1946- author
Title:	**The Practice of Love** ~ The Art of Growing in Greater Love of Yourself, Others and God
Description:	Maryville, TN : Ama Publishing [2024] Includes bibliographical references.
Identifiers:	LCCN 2023914317 — ISBN 978-0-9613176-3-8 (paperback) — ISBN 978-0-9613176-4-5 (e-book) — ISBN 978-0-9613176-5-2 (hardback)
Subjects:	1. Love 2. Spiritual Growth/Relationships 3. Christianity 4. Love of Self 5. Love of Others 6. Love of God 7. Personal Growth

Scripture quotations taken from the New American Standard Bible® (NASB), Copyright © 1960, 1962, 1963, 1968, 1971, 1972, 1973, 1975, 1977, 1995 by The Lockman Foundation. Used by permission. www.Lockman.org

Copyright © 2024 by Dave Beswick, Printed in the United States of America

All rights reserved.

No part of this book may be used or reproduced, stored in a retrieval system, or transmitted in any form or by any means—electronic, mechanical, photocopying, recording, or otherwise—without the prior written permission of the publisher. The only exception is brief quotations used in books, critical articles and reviews.

Requests to the Publisher for permission should be emailed to: dave@davebeswick.net

When the final bell tolls, the quality with which we have loved will stand out above all else as the gauge of a truly successful life.

What Others Are Saying About The Practice of Love

"So many people today are lost without a clue as to who they are and why they are here on this planet. This book offers a spiritual pathway that not only helps you discover your true identity and reason for being here, but also provides a panoply of choices to help you grow incrementally in greater love of God, others and yourself."

~ Dorothy Baudo, RN

"As a business person, I know the value of building strong relationships. This book has helped me grow these relationships by paying closer attention to the needs, wants, fears and frustrations of my employees and customers and then acting on what I hear with a 'How can I serve you?' attitude."

~ Charles Pusser, Chick-fil-A General Manager

"*The Practice of Love* is a clear and practical guidebook for how to go about fulfilling Jesus' greatest commandment to love God above all things and your neighbor as yourself."

~ Linda Carruthers,
Isaiah 117 House (Caring for children awaiting foster care)

"Going beyond the common intellectual and emotional ways of viewing love, Dave Beswick calls us to stop 'thinking about love' and to get down to the business of intentionally practicing it with a giving heart. If you are serious about growing in love, this three year work of love is a must read."

~ Fr. Charlie Donohue, CSP, Pastor

"Most of us throw the word love around but never take the time to spell out exactly what love means so that we can know if we are truly loving or not. As it turns out, love is not some mysterious or airy-fairy sort of thing that begs all definition, but rather a conscious choice and way of being in relationship that builds relationships up."

~ Olga Martin, Fitness Instructor

"*The Practice of Love* helped me see that when I lead with criticism people feel it immediately and turn away, but when I lead with love they come closer."

~ Carolyn Gentry, Tennis Instructor

"All through school we're taught how to read, write and speak, yet never how to listen empathetically, communicate compassionately and love from the heart. Herein lies the teaching to fill that gap."

~ Tina Wesson, Winner of *Survivor* (American TV Series)

"Dave Beswick unveils the anatomy of love in a way that leaves the reader with genuine hope and confidence that growing in greater love is within reach. Each chapter shows how love is a verb that involves our consistent participation in order to fulfill Christ's clarion call to 'Love one another.'"

~ Ryan Carter, Law Student

"Most people have preconceived ideas that love is a feeling, a strong sense of connection or a mystery that cannot be defined. They enter relationships hoping to find that elusive something called *love* that they hope will bring them a lifetime of fulfillment and happiness. Dave Beswick removes all elusiveness by clarifying what

love really means and offers practical ways to love even the most difficult of people."
~ Leon Dodd, Deacon

"Make it your conscious intention to bring the practice of love to everyone you meet and watch what happens."
~ Larry George, United States Marine Corps, Retired

"Want to have happy and meaningful relationships? Engage the practice of love on purpose, day in and day out, and your wish will be fulfilled. Dave Beswick has taken many paths on his spiritual journey, and has found that the love exemplified on the Jesus Path is the way to true happiness. When the Beatles sang 'All you need is love', it was a trite slogan; from the pen of Dave Beswick, it is a profound truism."
~ Bill Jacobs, Deacon

"Jesus accepted people where they were at and gently guided them to where God was calling them to be. He gave them the open space of love they needed to be able to hear the truth and the courage to act on what they heard. He invites us to do the same. This book teaches us the importance of accepting others as they are, listening to their needs, wants, fears and frustrations and responding with compassionate words and actions."
~ Fr. Pete Iorio, Pastor

"Dave Beswick conveys many profound points of view in language that can be clearly understood by the most common of individuals, like myself. I appreciate the way he uses his personal life experiences and those of others to bring his message to life. If you want a practical and inspiring book that helps you love more deeply, look no further."

~ Pat Thompson, Probation Officer

"We have a choice: To love in this moment or not. This book helps us see the difference."

~ Trevan McElroy, Chick-fil-A Director of Operations

"Eschewing abstract theological presentation, *The Practice of Love* teaches how to live authentic love. Firmly rooted in the mundane, which Christ has called us to sanctify, Beswick guides us in the many small daily decisions which conform the heart to Jesus and incarnate him within our lives."

~ Fr. Adam Royal, Associate Pastor

"Whether relating with our parents, siblings, relatives, in-laws, friends, co-workers, clients, customers, students, enemies or God, *The Practice of Love* provides the first gauge of its kind to help us assess how loving we are in our relationships and what changes we need to make in order to love better."

~ Patrick Meador, High School Music Teacher

Contents

Introduction 1

1. What Is the Practice of Love? 5
2. Why Engage the Practice of Love? 19
3. The Practice of Love and the Jesus Path 27
4. What Stands in the Way of Hearing the Truth? 37
5. The Ultimate Choice: Obey God or Chart Your Own Course 53
6. The Art of Growing in Greater Love of God 63
7. Seven Ways to Help Deepen Your Love of God 83
8. The Art of Growing in Greater Love of Yourself 95
9. Loving Your Enemies 125
10. The Art of Growing in Greater Love of Others 137
11. A Side-By-Side Comparison of When You Are and Are Not Engaging the Practice of Love with Others 167
12. Moving Forward ~ Cultivating the Art of Growing in Greater Love of Yourself, Others and God 173

Footnotes 181

Bibliography 187

About the Author: "A Life of Four Paths" 191

Index 193

In dedication and thanksgiving to...

my wife, Janie, for your unwavering love, patience, and trust and always putting family first.

my daughters, Noelle and Angelique, for the privilege of being your Dad, for being great kids and for laughing at my "Dad jokes."

my brother, Dan, for your generous love and support of our family when we needed it the most.

my dear friend, Pat Thompson, for your unselfish love of us, your wife, children and others. You inspire me each day to love the best I can knowing that I'll never love perfectly.

my fellow traveler on the path in search of authentic truth and love, Bernard Theroux, for your insights that have greatly impacted my life.

my mother-in-law, Janet Lydecker, for your consistent love and support of our family.

my spiritual mentor, Father Francis Rouleau, S.J., (1901-1984) for being Jesus' presence to me during my years in the seminary.

Introduction

As a longtime Jesuit seminarian, Buddhist practitioner and teacher of New Thought and Self-Help ideologies, I searched ardently for truth and love and what gave ultimate meaning and purpose to my life.

After becoming financially independent and then losing everything in a bad investment, I discovered a key in the Gospels that unlocked the door to loving better in all my relationships.

This one key, which took the form of a simple yet profound practice, opened the door to achieving peace of heart and happiness that I had never known before. I called this key the practice of love because love was shown to involve three specific actions to be engaged in relationship rather than merely an emotion to be felt.

The practice is not a technique in order to achieve some tangible result in a cause and effect sort of way. Rather, it is a way of being and acting in relationship that gradually enhances one's love of self, others and God.

As you are reading this book, you will recognize how you have engaged this practice often in your life without even knowing it and come to see how you can consciously employ it going forward to enhance every relationship in your life.

Since the practice of love is wholly compatible with the Jesus Path and is the road on which I have engaged the practice, I describe how one can practically grow in genuine love of self, others and God in the context of walking on this path.

However, while the Jesus Path is unique because it is all about relationship inspired by Jesus' greatest commandment to love God above all things and your neighbor as yourself, the practice can be engaged with great benefit no matter what your beliefs or where you are on your spiritual journey.

You may find it helpful to first read the book from cover to cover and then to go back and do a deeper dive into those chapters that draw your attention.

Here is a brief summary of the twelve chapters:

Chapter One, "What Is the Practice of Love?", explains what the practice of love is and gives many examples of the practice being lived out in everyday life.

Chapter Two, "Why Engage the Practice of Love?", offers the three main reasons for engaging the practice.

Chapter Three, "The Practice of Love and the Jesus Path", describes how Jesus engaged the practice with his Father and others and his invitation for everyone to follow his lead.

Chapter Four, "What Stands in the Way of Hearing the Truth?", reveals the main block from hearing the truth and discerning God's wishes for us in matters big and small.

Chapter Five, "The Ultimate Choice: Obey God or Chart Your Own Course", points out that we have been given free will to choose between right and wrong, truth and falsity and good and bad and that, in the end, it is our choices that determine the level of integrity we bring to the table.

Chapter Six, "The Art of Growing in Greater Love of God", reveals the main ways that the Spirit of truth speaks to us so that we can discern his voice, act on what we hear and thus grow in genuine love of God.

Chapter Seven, "Seven Ways to Help Deepen Your Love of God", offers meditative ways that have helped many over the centuries deepen their love of God.

Chapter Eight, "The Art of Growing in Greater Love of Yourself", presents the essential ingredients for growing in self-love and the importance of truly loving ourselves so that we will have more love to give and less problems in our relationships.

Chapter Nine, "Loving Your Enemies", responds to Jesus' countercultural call to love those who have done us wrong by helping us identify who our enemies are and how to go about loving and forgiving them for real.

Chapter Ten, "The Art of Growing in Greater Love of Others", teaches us that one of the primary ways to grow in love of others is by learning the lost art of listening and how to communicate effectively with others. It then guides us through six steps to become the best listener and communicator we can be.

Chapter Eleven, "A Side-By-Side Comparison of When You *Are* and *Are Not* Engaging the Practice of Love with Others", presents the first gauge of its kind to help us assess how loving we are and what changes we need to make in order to love better.

Chapter Twelve, "Moving Forward ~ Cultivating the Art of Growing in Greater Love of Yourself, Others and God", points out that it is our commitment to engage the practice of love each day that forms the foundation needed for love to survive and thrive in all our relationships.

About the Author, "A Life of Four Paths", presents an overview of the four paths that Dave Beswick has traveled as the context for writing this book.

ONE

What Is the Practice of Love?

The practice of love in the life of:

Pat

What I appreciate most about my close friend, Pat, is his ability to be with and bless people wherever they happen to be in the moment. No matter what he might be going through at the time, he repeatedly finds a way to let it go while allowing others the freedom to express themselves without judgment.

Throughout his life, Pat has demonstrated the genuine fulfillment that comes from giving and putting others first with a minimum of self-referencing.

To illustrate:

- ~ Since Janie and I adopted our two girls from China, he has sent both of them a yearly Christmas present of $25. This may not sound like a big deal, but it is to our girls. Someone they know only as "Pat", has simply been there for them without expecting anything in return.

~ His smudge paintings of Angelique with her beloved Shih-Tzu dog, Rocky, and of Noelle cheek-to-cheek with a llama in Peru, are true gifts of love that will remain with them as special keepsakes for the rest of their lives.

~ After hearing that we'd lost our life's savings in a bad investment, he did not hesitate for a second before sending a check to help us make it through the next two months.

~ Pat loved his wife, Jan, dearly. From the first time I saw them together until she passed away of cancer, he loved, appreciated and served her with a tender heart.

"Gram"

While living with us during my teenage years, my grandmother, affectionately known as "Gram", was consistently there with a listening ear and a calm and loving presence. She had an uncanny knack for being able to accept others and whatever was going on without getting overly upset or negatively judgmental. Her favorite saying, "This too shall pass", often helped me see that whatever I was getting upset about at the time would soon become a distant memory.

Whether being a wife, mom, performing duties for a housebound elderly woman for ten years or keeping house and being an emotional support during my adolescence, Gram steadily served others in a simple and unselfish way.

Janie

As one called to be "Mama", my wife, Janie, taught me the value of accepting and blessing our two girls where they were at in any given moment and that what they needed more than anything was our consistent love.

While the girls were going through the roller coaster ride of teenagehood, she helped me clarify the following unconscious pattern I had developed when relating with them:

- ~ Whenever they would say or do things I judged as being off, I would quickly react rather than respond by offering "constructive criticism" so that they might see better ways of speaking or acting in the future.

- ~ I believed, with good intention, that it was my duty as a father to bring them correction and insightful wisdom in those fiery moments whenever they said or did things that were off the mark. I wanted them to learn the lesson so that they hopefully would not repeat the same action down the road.

- ~ Over time, I saw how my reactive and critical approach in the heat of battle caused them to recoil. Whenever the "Here comes critical Daddy again" moments came along, they immediately felt criticized and unloved and pulled back like a cobra snake protecting itself against a predator.

~ Janie helped me see that if I kept being critical in the same way, that I would be in danger of losing my girls for good. I knew she was right.

~ She showed me through her actions that it was much more helpful to allow the girls to first play out their drama, knowing that no truth or insight could ever be heard while hysterical emotions were filling the air.

~ I came to see that the only way for them to be open to hearing any speck of truth would be by:

- Experiencing my consistent acceptance, warmth and love free of reactivity, cold critiques and judgmental stares.

- Trusting that I was there for them and that I enjoyed and loved them as they were no matter what awkward changes or reactive moods they happened to be going through at the time.

When going through a rough patch with our girls, Janie's best friend and mother of three, Laurel, offered this insight:

> "Kids in their teens and early twenties commonly think that their parents don't know much. You need to get used to the fact that they will love you one day and

wish they had different parents the next.

Understanding that hormones are most often leading the way, the key is to not take any of it personally and know that the developmental stage they are in now will not last forever—that they are really good girls and will eventually turn out just fine.

Never doubt for a moment that you are good parents and that what they want and need most of all is for you to be there for them and to feel your acceptance and love."

Like a mama bird caring for her chicks, Janie consistently pays close attention to the needs, wants, fears and frustrations of our girls and responds with a giving heart. She has a good sense of when one needs to stretch out on our bed and talk, play a game or watch a movie together.

When she needs to communicate with one of them about a sensitive matter, she usually picks the right time and place away from distractions and then speaks the truth to them in love.

Her sensitivity extends to her ninety-three year old mother who moved in with us two years ago on Christmas day. Whether making her coffee with special foam first thing in the morning, cooking her meals, driving her to doctors' appointments, managing her meds, helping her run errands, sharing a meal, watching TV together, talking about feelings and needs, rubbing her neck, back, legs or feet or going for a drive, she is there for her at her beck and call.

The practice of love in action also shows itself when:

- **A teacher** takes the time needed to develop a relationship and build trust with a struggling student until he accepts her invitation to meet before school and get the help he needs to get caught up with the rest of the class.

- **A hospice nurse** spends the last two weeks of Joe's life simply being there for him, giving him the space to say whatever he may be feeling or thinking. She simply listens with a compassionate heart as he talks about his year-long struggle with cancer, his worries about leaving his wife behind and what lies ahead after his death. Likewise, she empathetically feels the pain of his grieving wife and children and does her best to relieve some of their suffering.

- **A pastor,** despite being rather introverted, chooses to step out of his comfort zone and get to know his parishioners in order to identify their needs. After attending several parish functions, meeting with people over coffee and in their homes, talking to several others on the phone and conducting a written "Needs Survey", he then prayerfully considers ways to serve those needs.

- **An abused woman,** after attending group support meetings for close to nine months and developing trust within the group, now has the courage she needs to listen to her conscience and leave her abuser once and for all. She now has the resolve to start a new life, get regular counseling and continue with the group support that helped her arrive at this transformative time in her life.

~ **A man** accepts his overweight body without judgment and now wants to lose weight so that he can look and feel better and lead a healthier life. After reading about various diet regimens and why people choose to ingest some things and not others, he begins experimenting and listening closely to his body until he finds the diet that works best for him. He then responds by taking on the regimen and walking each day, not as a temporary weight loss effort, but as a lifestyle change, and feels genuinely good about himself for doing so. When he does eat off once in a while, he does not berate himself, but simply gets back on track and continues on.

~ **Two people** from different political parties accept each other as they are and engage in dialogue (= two people really talking) with a genuine desire of finding the truth. Acknowledging that they each have some beliefs that are firm and not open to alteration, they calmly address one political issue at a time sharing their views and why they think and feel as they do. They are open to the facts and speak about what they believe to be true while remaining open to discover new truths without clamoring for rebuttal or trying to change the other's viewpoint. They often respond by summarizing what they heard the other say so that both know they are being heard correctly.

~ **A woman,** after clarifying destructive patterns of behavior and communication that have been going on for years in her relationship, sits down with her husband to talk about it. While shaking in her boots not knowing what the outcome will be, she dares to share her feelings and thoughts and what she would like moving forward. She hopes that some truth or patterns of relating might be identified along with a desire by both of them to do whatever is needed to strengthen their relationship.

~ **A student** invites a girl eating by herself in the lunchroom to join her and her friends at their table.

~ **A salesman** takes the time needed to get to know his client so that he can identify his needs and wants and then do his best to meet those needs and wants as efficiently and cost-effectively as possible.

~ **A mother** spends a lot of quality time with her adopted daughter, knowing that it can often take many months and even years to build up trust when the fear of being left again (abandonment) is always close to the surface. Once trust has been built up, she makes it a point to consistently approach her with a positive, gentle and warm heart making it easier for her to open up whenever issues arise.

What, then, are the 3 main actions involved when engaging the practice of love with others?

The practice of love involves building trust by:

1. **WELCOMING and ACCEPTING** others as they are, being fully and calmly present and providing a compassionate and expanded space of openness and warmth for them to speak freely and be themselves without fear of being judged or given unsolicited advice.

2. **LISTENING** empathetically to what they are saying, needing, wanting and feeling with open eyes, an open mind and a softened heart.

3. **RESPONDING** to what you hear with a "How can I serve you?" attitude.

As you read through this book, you will learn how to incrementally deepen your love of others as well as what you can practically do to grow in greater love of God and yourself.

The practice of love in action also shows itself when:

~ **A social worker** makes a strong connection with a woman in a homeless shelter. Over the course of two months she spends quality time with the woman to the point where trust is built up. Feeling listened to and accepted for who she is, she tells the social worker that she would like to get a part-time job as the first step on her road to eventually getting a place of her own. After listening attentively to her needs as well as her fears, she helps her find her first job in five years.

~ **A couple** sits down and begins talking about her aging father who is getting to the point where he will soon not be able to live on his own without getting extra help. Reflecting on the commandment to honor thy father and thy mother (which originally meant to take care of your parents in their old age), they decide that they will invite her father to move in with them so that he can be cared for by family if, and only if, he feels like that is something he would like to do. They meet with her father and begin the conversation about how he would like to live going forward. After listening compassionately to his spoken and unspoken words, they get the clear message that he wants to stay in his own house for as long as he can before considering making a move.

He said that he would like to continue driving for as long as he can while referring to his trusted car as his "freedom machine." He also said that he would like someone to come in and help him with certain things like cleaning the house, doing some shopping and driving him to events or restaurants in the evening because night driving was hard for him.

After telling her father that he was welcome to move in with them whenever he no longer could or wished to live alone, he was extremely grateful. "I never want to go into an assisted living situation unless I absolutely have to," he said. Thus, with his permission, they began looking for caregivers to serve his spoken needs.

~ **A woman** brings consistent positive and loving energy to a fellow employee who continually shows little empathy, care or concern for her or anyone else.

~ **A father** makes it a point to connect with his son often during his teenage years in order to build a strong and trusting relationship. He wants to be a steady presence in his life and be someone that his son can talk to about anything whether it be about school, friends, dating, religious stuff, hobbies, work or college.

He thus carves out regular time to spend with his son whether it be attending his games, watching a movie together or going on hikes or out to eat. He often asks him questions to get the conversation going and then calmly listens without interrupting. He frequently repeats back in his own words what he heard him saying to help him clarify his thoughts or decision making. When he does speak to his son, he makes it a point to be as supportive and upbeat as he can and offers his wise input only in short spurts when the opening presents itself.

The practice of love is also about being and basking in the presence of those we love and hold most dear, including our animals.

Love is the act of welcoming others as they are, listening to them with open eyes and ears and then responding to what we hear with a serving heart. It is wishing the best for them as well. It is also about allowing ourselves to just be and bask in the presence and love of those we hold most dear. For this enjoyment to take place, we bring our busyness to a halt, shut down our electronic screens and simply delight in the presence of those whom we call family and friends.

Whether eating, playing, chatting, laughing at jokes, telling jokes, praying, being in nature, being on vacation, listening to music, riding in the car, playing a board game, worshipping, watching a movie or savoring the smells of breakfast being cooked on the stove, we are simply present and soak in the love that is felt when we are all together.

It is having occasional disagreements and working through them without hard feelings. It is being a teacher one moment and a student the next. It is missing others when they're gone and joyfully welcoming them when they walk through the door. It is thousands of beautiful gestures.

Enjoying and loving our animals is also part of the quilt of love that envelops our lives. For example, most mornings our Shih-Tzu dog, Rocky, jumps off of the bed, walks out into the hallway and then rolls onto his back with his tail thumping on the carpeted floor waiting for his tummy to be rubbed. Bringing a smile to my face and heart by his warm presence, I typically greet him with "Good morning Rocky boy—good morning buddy! You're my good boy—I love you so much."

Dogs have the first part of the practice of love down pat by being fully and happily present in the moment and showing unconditional regard no matter if they smell another dog on your leg or not. With tails wagging and often an excited bark at seeing you as if you'd been away for a month, they make you feel like you are the coolest and best thing to ever walk through the door. They make you smile, act like a little kid and feel good all over.

Imagine what the world would be like if we all greeted each other like our dogs greeted us. "According to Megan Daley Olmert, the director of research at Warrior Canine Connection, who has worked in the field of biology of the human-animal bond for over 30 years, oxytocin [a peptide hormone and neuropeptide] plays a crucial role in social bonding and brain function. We now know that whenever you look at your dog, talk to your dog in a high-pitched, positive way, pet your dog, brush your dog or are involved in a loving and social way with your dog, you're releasing oxytocin," Olmert explained.[1]

The practice of love also comes into play whenever we listen to our animals and respond to their needs in loving service. For example, when Rocky scratches his side, it usually means that it's time for his flea and tick medicine, while pawing at the front door means that he has to poop with little time to spare.

We also love him by taking him for rides in the car, going for walks, throwing his favorite toy to chase and delighting when he sits on his hind legs begging for food or rests his head on a soft pillow while sleeping.

TWO

Why Engage the Practice of Love?

Three Reasons:

1. Love is eternal. [1]

The love we are talking about here is agape love, or the unconditional and eternal love that God has for us from the time he formed us in our mother's womb. We are talking about a love that is absolute and always forgives and takes us back no matter what we might think, say or do that is less than loving.

In contrast,

- ~ Everything else we can see, touch, taste, smell or hear is temporary.
  - Every person, thing, experience, thought, bodily feeling and emotion that comes into form gradually changes and eventually passes away.

- All pleasures last only as long as the pleasurable activities themselves.
- Even the stars, planets and sun have a limited life span and the biggest bolder in the world will eventually turn to dust.

~ All human distinctions and all that we have accumulated during our lives in terms of:

> occupations
> possessions
> money
> family
> friends
> knowledge
> personal talents
> awards
> degrees
> ranks
> positions
> enjoyable experiences
>
> and the reputation, image and status we have built up over the years,
>
> must be left at death's door.

If there is no God, then seeking passing pleasures and avoiding pain becomes a viable life-purpose. On the other hand, if love is eternal as St. Paul says, and God is love as St. John asserts, then growing in greater love of God and our neighbor while on earth becomes the ultimate treasure worth striving for.

2. It makes us most happy.

> "I don't know what your destiny will be, but one thing I know: the only ones among you who will be really happy are those who will have sought and found how to serve." [2]
>
> ~ Albert Schweitzer

The First Noelle

When Janie and I were first dating, it was all about meeting our own needs and wants, enjoying the titillating feelings that came with the infatuation phase and basically doing whatever pleasurable activities struck our fancy. Whether playing tennis, going to movies, dining out, going for walks or traveling to fun places, the focus of our attention was primarily on ourselves.

After getting married, Janie continued bringing up her heartfelt wish to adopt two Asian girls, a desire that took root in her when she was seventeen. Having had a less than glorious family experience growing up, I was initially resistant to the idea of bringing children into the mix. I did not want to give up the enjoyable thing we had going. After finally letting go of my resistance, two years later we were on our way to China to pick up baby Noelle. Two years after that, we made the long journey once again and welcomed four-year-old Angelique into the fold.

With the onset of family, I think God plays a trick on us. He gets us all revved up in the romantic love phase which usually leads to marriage and children in pretty short order. Then, once a child appears on the scene, we immediately get thrust into the sacrificial love phase where we are forced, whether we like it or not, to put someone else before ourselves. By so doing, we are given the opportunity to learn the art of loving that Jesus embodied by constantly laying down our life for our children and our mate.

> The family is a school of love where we learn to put others before ourselves and give from the heart.

After purchasing a state-of-the-art crib for Noelle that had a pull-down side, making it easy to put her in and take her out of the crib, we went in to check on her that evening and found that she had climbed completely out of the crib and was playing on the floor. After one more climbing incident, she made it crystal clear that the crib was not for her—that she preferred sleeping on the carpeted floor.

Before we knew what hit us, sacrificial love was in full swing with both of us taking turns sleeping with her on the floor. Over the next three months, each night she would doze off to sleep in her green, toddler-sized sleeping bag, hearing one of us read her favorite bedtime story, *Good Night Moon*.

Once the sleeping on the floor period came to an end, Noelle was happy going to sleep in her new, red fire truck bed. Grateful to be back in our own bed, Janie and I regularly got up in the middle of the night to feed, change diapers or comfort someone having a bad dream. When Noelle went through a six-month colicky and crying phase due to health problems and never getting off of China time, Janie did not hesitate doing the only thing that would stop her crying—going on long car rides three to four times a week.

Without realizing it, WE were no longer #1. By putting

Noelle and Angelique first and doing the playful and fun things that parents do with their children, life was quite enjoyable.

After several more years of parenthood, we gradually came to realize that the only way to make the whole family thing work was if we both put each other and our children first. Laying down our lives in this way did not mean that romance or meeting our own needs were no longer important, but that we were genuinely happier when serving and giving.

Parents who unselfishly care for their children each day know intimately what sacrificial love is all about. Whether getting up at night to chase away a monster, rising early to prepare the day's schedule, making breakfast and washing clothes before the kids ever awaken, their focus is on serving the needs of their family.

Afterwards they do more things like changing sheets, vacuuming, shopping, paying bills, arranging for pickups, caring for their own parents, attending school events, making home improvements, helping with homework, playing games, going to birthday parties and, oh yes, working to earn money in order to provide food, shelter and clothing.

As the kids get older, they become professional chauffeurs driving them to practice, part-time jobs and fun places like tennis courts, athletic fields, movies, the mall and the park. Did I mention that they buy lots of stuff for their kids along the way like trikes, bikes, skates, skis, bats, balls, uniforms, and memberships to zoos, clubs, and amusement parks and go on day trips and vacations? Then they engage the process of helping them decide what the next best step for them might be after high school and then support their decisions by assisting in any way they can.

Instead of spending their lives waiting to be given to, entertained and served by others, they feel the true peace and joy that comes when they choose to listen empathetically and respond in loving service over and over again.

Parenthood is not the only vocation, of course, that can teach us the value of sacrificial love—that can confirm St. Francis' felt experience that "It is in giving that we receive." When others are put in serving situations like at work or when helping a young person, serving a needy parent, volunteering at a food bank or giving of their time, treasure and talent for the service of others, they too come to realize that they are most happy when serving rather than being served—that genuine fulfillment comes from putting others first.

3. It enhances the quality of all our relationships.

When we consistently engage the practice of love with:

- ~ God, our relationship with God grows.

- ~ Our mate, our relationship grows as a couple.

- ~ Our children, parents, siblings, relatives and in-laws, our love grows as a family.

- ~ Our friends and those in our church and social groups, our relationships grow in the community.

- ~ Our boss, co-workers, employees, clients, patients, students and customers in our work, our work relationships are strengthened and the more productive and profitable our work becomes.

~ Ourselves, we grow in genuine self-love and thus have more love to give in our relationships.

THREE

The Practice of Love and the Jesus Path

A. Jesus engaged the practice of love with others.

Jesus welcomed and accepted people where they were at and gently guided them to where God was calling them to be. Zacchaeus was one of those people. As a chief tax-collector at Jericho working for the Roman Empire rather than the Jewish community, he was scorned as a corrupt traitor. Here is the story of his encounter with Jesus:

> "Jesus entered Jericho and was passing through. A man was there by the name of Zacchaeus; he was a chief tax collector and was wealthy. He wanted to see who Jesus was, but because he was short he could not see over the crowd. So he ran ahead and climbed a sycamore-fig tree to see him since Jesus was coming that way.

When Jesus reached the spot, he looked up and said to him, 'Zacchaeus, come down immediately. I must stay at your house today.'

So he came down at once and welcomed him gladly. All the people saw this and began to mutter, 'He has gone to be the guest of a sinner.'

But Zacchaeus stood up and said to the Lord, 'Look, Lord! Here and now I give half of my possessions to the poor, and if I have cheated anybody out of anything, I will pay back four times the amount.'

Jesus said to him, 'Today salvation has come to this house, because this man, too, is a son of Abraham. For the Son of Man came to seek and to save the lost.'" [1]

Rather than condemning him as a sinner, Jesus looked at him, called him by name and told him to come down for he intended to visit his house. In contrast to those who judged him as wrong for dining with such a low-life, Jesus accepted Zacchaeus as he was. He gave him the open space of love he needed to be able to see the truth and boldly say that he would give half of his possessions to the poor and pay back those he cheated four times over.

The gentleness of Jesus was also given to the Samaritan woman who met Jesus at the well during the hottest time of day, a time when her naysayers would not likely be around to jeer at her for her many marriages. Instead of criticizing her for having had six husbands, he tells her that he is the living water and moves her heart to drink of this water so that she will never be spiritually thirsty again. [2]

By accepting and connecting with Zacchaeus and the woman at the well with his love and forgiveness, Jesus gave the world an important message:

> ~ It is only when we compassionately accept, welcome and bless others as they are and listen to them with a softened heart, that they may be open to see the truth, love in a similar way or choose to make a positive change in their lives.

B. Jesus engaged the practice of love with his Father.

For Jesus, it was all about relationship. When asked what the greatest commandment in the Law was and later on how someone could inherit eternal life, Jesus replied:

> "**Love** the Lord your God with **all** your heart and with **all** your soul and with **all** your mind. This is the *first* and greatest commandment. And the second is like it: **Love** your neighbor as yourself. All the Law and the Prophets hang on these two commandments." [3]

For Jesus, loving God with **all** your heart, soul and mind came first which naturally overflowed into service of others. How did Jesus go about loving his Father?

The answer to this question comes from looking at Jesus' own purpose in life and how he went about fulfilling it.

Jesus came to do the will of his Father—to teach and demonstrate the truth. Everything he said and did came from the core relationship with the one he called "Abba." Doing the will of Abba and testifying to the truth was the purpose of his life. In Jesus' own words,

> ". . . I have come from heaven, not to do my own will, but to do the will of the one who sent me." [4]

> ". . . the world must be brought to know that I love the Father and that I am doing exactly what the Father told me." [5]

> "For this I was born and for this I came into the world, to testify to the truth. Everyone who belongs to the truth listens to my voice." [6]

For Jesus, Abba was the truth and the source and revealer of all truth. He was the only one who could truly guide. While his mother, Mary, undoubtedly knew his heart more than anyone else, only Abba could bring him true peace, clarity and comfort during times of immense stress and ridicule. Abba was his constant companion, sharing his every experience, thought, feeling and bodily pain. During his three years of ministry, only Abba was there guiding him each step of the way to speak and manifest the truth in love.

For Jesus, loving God with his whole heart, soul and mind was synonymous with doing his Father's will.

How, then, did he come to know his will?

To know the will of the Father, he had to do one important thing: **listen**. As he was about to begin his public ministry, for instance, he went up to the mountain and spent the night in prayer. Afterward, he came down and chose his twelve apostles. He **listened** to his Father first with the ear of the heart, made a big decision and then **acted** on what he heard.

Whether alone on a hill, being baptized by John in the river Jordan or walking amidst the people, Jesus would **listen** to the Father and then **respond** in loving service of others. He would engage the practice of love not as a three-step method, but as a personal relationship with his Father and everyone he met.

It was in the Garden of Gethsemane where he begged his Father to take the cup of impending suffering away from him if it was his will. ". . . Abba, Father", he said, "all things are possible to you. Take this cup away from me. But not what I will, but what you will." [7]

His Father did **not** take the cup away from him. While sweating blood and with every cell in his body urging him not to do his Father's will, he resisted the temptation. With the sins of the world past, present and future pressing down upon him, he listened and then acted on what he heard by going through horrible suffering and death for the love of humankind. He was obedient unto death so that everyone would be saved from being eternally alienated from God, others and themselves.

By listening daily to his Father and then acting faithfully on what he heard, he showed what it means to love God with all your heart, all your soul and all your mind. He demonstrated that sacrificial love, or the laying down of one's life for one's friends, is the highest form of love.

"No one has greater love than this, to lay down one's life for one's friends." ~ Jn. 15:13

C. Jesus urged everyone to engage the practice of love.

Inseparably linked with Jesus' primary focus on doing the will of the Father, was his strong urging that everyone else do the will of the Father in heaven as well by **listening** to his words and **acting** on what they hear.

> "It is not those who say to me, 'Lord, Lord', who will enter the kingdom of heaven, but the person who *does* the will of my Father in heaven." [8]

> Jesus describes his true disciple as one who" ...*listens* to my words and *acts* on them." [9]

> "Therefore, everyone who listens to these words of mine and acts on them will be like a sensible man who built his house on rock... And everyone who *listens* to these words of mine and does not *act* on them will be like a fool who built his house on sand." [10]

And then there was Mary who chose to listen to Jesus instead of resentfully scurrying about doing things like her sister Martha:

> "In the course of their journey he came to a village, and a woman named Martha

welcomed him into her house. She had a sister called Mary, who sat down at the Lord's feet and **listened to him speaking.**

Now Martha who was distracted with all the serving said, 'Lord, do you not care that my sister is leaving me to do the serving all by myself? Please tell her to help me.'

But the Lord answered: 'Martha, Martha, you worry and fret about so many things and yet few are needed, indeed only one. It is Mary who has chosen the better part; it is not to be taken from her.' " [11]

Jesus looked at Martha with love and gently told her that listening to him was more important than making sure everyone had something to eat. Through this intimate encounter, he revealed the truth that listening to him and being in alignment with his will was the easiest way of achieving true peace and happiness on earth. It is no wonder, then, why Jesus asked us to pray "Thy will be done" in the only prayer he taught in the gospels:

> "Pray, then, in this way:
> Our Father who art in heaven,
> Hallowed be Thy name.
> Thy kingdom come,
> ***Thy will be done,***
> On earth as it is in heaven." [12]

Doing the will of his Father was so important to Jesus that he said that his will is to be done not only on earth but in heaven as well. If doing our best to consistently listen to the Father in loving service is what brings us true peace and happiness on earth, will we not experience a far deeper peace and joy by being in his presence, listening to him and doing his will in heaven?

It is intriguing to contemplate what doing his will in heaven might entail. For example, might it involve:

- ~ Taking care of unfinished business before coming into his presence by becoming aware of and overcoming our negative habits of mind, heart and body and thus learning the lessons we failed to learn on earth?
- ~ Being a guardian angel for others by watching over them, praying for them, nudging them to see the truth in whatever relationship or circumstance they are in and then encouraging them to respond by doing what is right for themselves and others?
- ~ Ecstatically praising and worshipping God with all the angels and saints in celebration of his will being done in heaven and on earth?

Summary

Jesus taught and demonstrated a unique way of being and acting in relationship to help us and others grow in love. It is the way of:

- ~ Compassionately welcoming, accepting and blessing others as they are and listening to them free of righteous judgment, so that we may be open to see the light of truth, love in a similar way and begin making changes for the better.

~ Seeking to do the Father's will in big things and in small by **listening** to him with the ear of the heart and then **responding** to what we hear in loving service over and over again.

Jesus gave us his Greatest Commandment to love God above all things and our neighbor as ourselves not to make life miserable for us, but to make us truly happy. He knew that whenever we did our best to listen to him and then respond by utilizing our talents for the service of others, that we would be genuinely happy as a result. By obeying the will of his Father throughout his life on earth even to death on a cross, he showed us the way to to true happiness, peace and joy.

But, how do we go about discerning his will? What are the main avenues through which he speaks so that we can do our best to listen to him and act on what we hear? Before we can answer these questions, we must first become aware of what it is that stands in the way of hearing the truth and discerning God's wishes for us.

FOUR

What Stands in the Way of Hearing the Truth?

To set the stage for this consideration, notice that whenever Jesus:

- ~ Healed the sick or forgave sins, he was in one place and often dealt with only one person at a time.

- ~ Preached to the crowds or taught his apostles, he was in one place speaking to one group at a time.

Prior to his death, he said that he had to go in order for him to send the Holy Spirit (i.e., for everyone, not only for one person or one group at a time). His plan was not simply to live with us but in us. He was confident that we could have a personal relationship with the Holy Spirit and that we could be guided by that same Spirit each day of our lives.

> "But I tell you the truth, it is better for you that I go. For if I do not go, the Advocate

> [the Holy Spirit] will not come to you. But if I go, I will send him to you." [1]

Jesus did go and did send the Holy Spirit to remind everyone of all that Jesus said and did and to guide them to all truth. In Jesus' words:

> "I have much more to tell you, but you cannot bear it now. But when he comes, the Spirit of truth will guide you to all truth." [2]

> "... and the truth will set you free." [3]

Thus, it is our role to learn and absorb as much of Jesus' words and teachings as possible so that we can be reminded of them more easily in our relationships and the affairs of daily living. The Holy Spirit not only guides us to remember what Jesus said and did, but also warns us, encourages us and speaks to us through our conscience guiding us always to do what is right, true and good.

Taking Jesus at his word, the Holy Spirit did not stop speaking with the death of the last apostle or when the last word was penned in the New Testament, but rather still has much more to say and much more guiding to do.

Before we can hear what the Spirit is saying, we first need to clarify what we do that blocks the truth from breaking through. This chapter gives us the opportunity to clarify what that block is.

A. The rich man's obstacle

> "As Jesus was setting out again, a man ran up to him, knelt down in front of him, and asked him, 'Good Teacher, what must I do

to inherit eternal life?'

'Why do you call me good?' Jesus asked him. 'Nobody is good except for one — God. You know the commandments: 'Never murder.' 'Never commit adultery.' 'Never steal.' 'Never give false testimony.' 'Never cheat.' 'Honor your father and mother.'

The man replied to him, 'Teacher, I have obeyed all of these since I was a young man.'

Jesus looked at him and loved him. Then he told him, 'You're missing one thing. Go and sell everything you own, give the money to the destitute, and you will have treasure in heaven. Then come back and follow me.'

Shocked at this statement, the man went away sad, because he had many possessions." [4]

What do you think was the main obstacle that blocked him from hearing the truth and responding to what he heard? Consider this:

He was a wealthy man, probably tithed more money to the synagogue than the required amount and gave regularly of his time and talents to help others. He no doubt had a certain status in the community that he enjoyed and was likely proud of what he had accomplished, what he knew about his field of endeavor and the wealth and possessions that he had amassed. After all, it had probably taken him many long years to build up his work, possessions and reputation, and didn't want to let it go—even at the cost of losing heaven.

Jesus was not saying that being wealthy and having possessions was what caused him to be closed to hearing the truth. Rather, he was calling him to let go of his identification with his wealth and possessions and the status, reputation and pride that came with it, and become his disciple. He was inviting him to surrender what was temporary for the sake of obtaining the eternal.

Notice that Jesus looked at him and loved him before he told him what he needed to do to have treasure in heaven. He knew that the rich man must first feel his love before he would ever be motivated to change and chart a new course. Yet, even with Jesus looking directly at him and loving him, it was not enough to move his heart to follow him. The attachment to and identification with what he possessed and the hard-fought image and reputation he had built up, was simply too strong. Did he eventually have a change of heart and return to follow Jesus? We do not know.

The key message from this story is that the obstacle of identifying with one's image and reputation can become extremely powerful once it takes hold. It is precisely this act of identifying with anything at all as equal to who we are, and any pride that accompanies it, that keeps us closed off from the truth and influence of God.

B. Part one of our lives is spent building our identity and reputation.

We come into this world as a child of God without any specific image or identity. We arrive without any beliefs, knowledge, degrees, titles, possessions, work or groups with which to identify.

Then, during the first part of our lives, through our interaction with and support of our parents, religious educators, teachers, individuals in our cultural milieu and through the powerful influence of advertising, the media and cultural conditioning, we gradually identify with, as equal to who we are, one or more identities and the reputation that goes along with it.

Our identity and reputation is not only how we see ourselves, but also how others see us, know us and relate to us. Sometimes our identity and reputation are attached to what we do, the roles we play, what we own, how much we are worth or what level of success we've achieved in the world. It may also be attached to what we know or believe and to prestigious letters that come before or after our name.

It may even be associated with the rank or position we've achieved, who or what we have control over or who we know. Perhaps we have become an expert in our field, or at least one of the most knowledgeable or experienced, which adds to our ability to make a good impression.

This labeling process gives us a way of identifying ourselves as a particular someone in a world which demands names and labels in order to differentiate and categorize. It enables us to say to ourselves and others, "this is who I am."

By being able to say things like, "I am or I was a teacher, nurse, counselor, salesperson, artist, writer, professor, engineer, parent, manager or a member of this or that religion, group or political party," we are given a sense of belonging and fitting in. Once we have our identity at least somewhat in place, we can finally breathe a sigh of relief that we won't be left speechless when asked what we do or what we did.

We've worked hard for our image and reputation and don't want to lose it.

During the first part of our lives, which can last a lifetime, we spend most of our efforts building up, protecting and preserving our identity and the reputation that accompanies it. This desire to be seen in a positive light is something we do mechanically rather than arriving at this aspiration after thoughtful consideration.

While steering our own ship, we strive with all our might to make a name for ourselves and to maintain our position in the world. It may be a relatively humble position, but it is ours nonetheless, and we do not want to lose it. We can identify with and be proud of a non-prestigious job or role just as easily as we can with being the CEO of a company.

In an effort to be loved, admired and respected, we avoid anything that will jeopardize our social standing and the image we have built up in our own minds. As a result, we tend to listen only to those voices that encourage us to maintain our fleeting identity as it is. Having built our identity house on sand, we then do all we can to prevent others, including God, from blowing it down.

Why do we hold on so tightly to our identity and reputation?

Could it be that we fear:

- ~ Hearing the truth about who God wants us to be, what he wants us to do and what it will ask of us?

- ~ Losing our familiar circle of friends, associates, clients, customers, patients or students?

- ~ That the day-to-day life as we have known it will come to an end?

~ Having to start all over again with apparently little or no support coming our way?

This clinging to our identity and reputation in part one of our lives does not mean that while going through this initial stage we:

~ Do not have a relationship with God.

~ Never listen to God or hear any truth.

~ Do not learn important life lessons and make some needed changes along the way.

Rather, it means that in part one *we* are primarily the navigators of our own boat with *my will be done* being the main sail that directs our course. It is not until part two of our lives, if and when it arrives, that we gradually, and not without some resistance, let God take over the helm until *Thy will be done* becomes the rudder and the motivation that guides our life.

C. How do we go about forming our identity and reputation?

Our identity and reputation are formed by identifying with, as equal to who we are, any combination from the list below. As you read over the following list, check off the ones with which you tend to identify and add any to the list that are not included here:

___	**Occupation**	*(what I do)*
___	**Role**	*(what role I play)*
___	**Rank or Position**	*(what rank or position I've achieved)*
___	**Beliefs**	*(what I believe: i.e., personally, politically, spiritually)*
___	**Knowledge**	*(what I know or the specialized knowledge I've aquired)*

The Practice of Love

___ Titles, Degrees (what prestigious letters I have before/after my name)
___ Power (what and who I have control over)
___ Possessions (what I own)
___ Money (what I am are worth)
___ Success (what level of success I've achieved)
___ Goals achieved (what personal and business goals I've achieved)
___ Social class (what social class I belong to)
___ Place of residence (where I live and/or the house I live in)
___ Culture (what culture I am a part of)
___ Race (what race I belong to)
___ Contacts (who I know and hang out with)
___ Personality traits (what I act like)
___ Appearance (what I look like)
___ Gender (what gender I identify with)
___ Sexual orientation (what sexual orientation I embrace)

The bottom line is that when we cling to any one or more of the above as equal to who we are and the reputation that goes with it, and ward off anyone who opposes fostering a continuance of this reputation, the Spirit of truth cannot get in. Also, when we identify with a particular point of view, any facts to the contrary are not allowed to penetrate.

Do you know people who seem to be identified with and proud of what:

~ They do or the important roles they play?

~ They own or the amount of money or possessions they have?

~ Their political beliefs are and thus become personally offended when you disagree with any of these beliefs?

- Their spiritual beliefs are and leave no room for dialogue that might shed new light, truth or insight?

- Their cultural heritage or race happens to be?

- They look like or who or what they know?

- Social class they belong to?

D. Some identities I've created or assumed over the course of my life.

Until later in life, all of my pursuits were connected with unconsciously building up and identifying with an idealized image or false self. Each self gave me a different label and reputation on which to hang my hat during my life's journey. In an effort to be liked, respected and loved by myself and others, each one made me feel like a special someone.

Usually fantasizing about something I would be doing in the future like writing books, giving workshops and retreats and teaching popular classes, I saw myself being recognized and esteemed as a knowledgeable expert in my field. By leaving books, courses, videos and recordings of my work behind, I even imagined being immortalized or permanently remembered long after I was dead and gone.

The list below contains some of the main "I ams" or identities with which I identified and built my reputation around during the first part of my life. As you read along, feel free to make an "I am" list of your own.

I am a baseball player.

I first sought after love and glory by becoming one of the top twelve high school baseball players in California. With a scrapbook full of newspaper articles chronicling my baseball prowess, I identified with being a baseball player.

After receiving a baseball scholarship to a university that had been to the college world series the year before, I was hitting the ball extremely well when I got hit by a pitch breaking a bone in my left hand. One errant pitch brought my season and career to an untimely end.

Needless to say, I was devastated. For the first time, I felt like a rower without a paddle — without any sense of identity, purpose and direction in my life. If I wasn't a baseball player, then who was I?

After that, I identified with being a:

- ~ Catholic Christian.
- ~ Jesuit seminarian.
- ~ Teacher with an M.A. in Religious Education.
- ~ Counselor, coach and retreat giver.

I am a funny guy and imitator.

Another way I sought to be liked and loved was trying to be funny and doing imitations. While I was a teacher, counselor and coach at a parochial high school in Bellevue, Washington, one year I was in charge of the Easter chocolate drive to raise money for our service program.

Each morning before recess, I would come on the loudspeaker for ten minutes as the "Funny Bunny" and pretend to interview famous people who always had a humorous and motivational message for the students encouraging them to sell more chocolate bars.

This daily interlude of comic relief was a big hit. While I was gifted at being able to imitate the voices of famous people, I was also identified with being a funny guy and imitator and the students and staff all gladly fed this persona.

Whether teaching, coaching or giving retreats, this false self would consistently come through seeking to get laughs and acceptance from whatever audience happened to be listening.

The next year I repeated the same gig, but the response was totally different. When I showed up in the gym in my Funny Bunny costume at the end of the chocolate drive, all the seniors had paper bags over their heads in protest of the whole fake Funny Bunny schtick. Having been so identified with my funny guy persona, I felt mortified. My false self was no longer being fed, leaving me hungry for the acceptance and validation that I had received the year before.

In short, my life was one big karaoke night where I was more comfortable imitating other people than being the real me.

Moving on from there, I identified with being a:

- ~ Worker amongst the Spanish speaking poor.
- ~ Certified Intensive Journal consultant and workshop giver helping people grow in self-understanding and their relationships through the power of journal writing.

~ Buddhist practitioner and teacher hoping to one day become enlightened or totally one in my essence with the universal light or consciousness (= I am light, consciousness or god).

~ Compiler of a 5 volume reference guide on Eastern teaching.

~ Workshop giver of New Thought and Self-Help ideologies.

~ Writer and promoter of two best-selling self-help/humor books.

To the extent that I identified with any of these temporary identities and the reputation that went along with them, and pushed away anyone who encouraged me to be the real me instead, the Spirit of truth could not get in.

Now let us look at how identifying with negative beliefs about ourselves and with the negative emotions of fear, sorrow and anger can also stand in the way of hearing God's truth and call.

E. The identities of Moses in the form of negative beliefs

God appeared to Moses at the burning bush and called him to lead the children of Israel out of Egyptian bondage. In response, Moses gave excuses as to why he did not think he was the man for the job. Being identified with his negative beliefs that he was not **good enough** presented a formidable obstacle making it difficult for him to hear and trust what God was asking of him.

His negative beliefs were:

- I am a lowly shepherd. (= I am not skilled enough.)
- I am too old for this job. I mean, I'm 80 years old, way past the average life span for my generation. And besides, I haven't been to Egypt in forty years!
- I am not knowledgeable enough to answer the questions the Israelites will have for me.
- I am afraid they will not listen. In response, God got the people to listen by giving Moses a rod that turned into a serpent, making his own hand turn into leprosy and turning water into blood.
- I am slow in speech and slow of tongue. In response, God said not to worry and sent his brother, Aaron, along to help him out. He also called him to get over his fearful identity of being a stutterer. [5]

As described in the book of Acts centuries later, here's what was said about this person who claimed to be clumsy with words: "Moses was taught all the wisdom of the Egyptians, and he became mighty in both speech and action." [6] God not only worked through Moses, but changed him in the process.

F. What negative beliefs do you have that are keeping you stuck?

The Practice of Love

Do you have something that you feel strongly moved or called to do but, like Moses, your mind keeps coming up with reasons why you can't do it? In other words, do you also have negative beliefs that you've accepted as true and identify with that are preventing you from bringing God's wishes for you to fruition?

To clarify what these beliefs are, check off any of the following that ring true and add any others to the list that come to you.

At this point in my life, I believe that **I am not**:

___ Skilled enough.
___ Experienced enough.
___ Educated, knowledgeable or trained enough; that I will not be accepted or respected unless I have an advanced degree or specialized training.
___ Ready enough; I've got to get everything perfectly in order before I get out there.
___ Good enough yet and need to prove myself first.
___ Likable and lovable enough.
___ Creative enough.
___ Good at speaking in public or talking on the phone.
___ Outgoing or energetic enough.
___ Worthy of forgiveness and success due to my past failings.
___ Confident, strong, powerful, or secure within myself enough.
___ Healthy enough.

At this moment, I believe that **I am not**:

___ Financially stable enough to begin or sustain this work. For example:
"I want to do God's will, but I just can't afford it." Or,
"I can't begin my calling in earnest until all my loans are paid off."

___ Able to maintain the consistent focus it takes to be successful.
___ Able to move forward because I have a learning or other disability.
___ Able to change, get out of my rut or do something different than I've done in the past; it is better to play it safe and keep doing what is familiar.
___ Able to carve out the time needed amidst all my responsibilities.

Thus, the act of identifying with any negative belief as equal to who you are puts a limit on your ability to listen to the Spirit of truth and discern your call.

Here are three steps to go beyond negative beliefs:

1. Become aware of them and see how they are preventing you from carrying out your calling.
2. Realize that if God is calling you, you have everything you need *right now* to fulfill that calling.
3. Take action towards fulfilling your calling one step at a time.

G. How identifying with fear, sorrow or anger can close the door to truth.

There are legitimate reasons for feeling fear, sorrow and anger. For example, feeling afraid when in the presence of a hurricane, feeling sad when a loved one dies or feeling angry when unjustly treated by another, are all warranted reasons to have these feelings.

However, when we identify with and become any of these emotions for a short or longer period of time, we close the door to hearing the truth. As long as we are locked up in the prison cell of our fear, sorrow or anger, the Spirit of truth cannot get in. For example, when we identify with and literally become:

Afraid (= "I am afraid"), we become frozen in our tracks.
Sad   (= "I am sad"), we shut down in the heart.
Angry (= "I am angry!"), we push others and the truth away.

Thus, when feelings of fear, sorrow or anger arise in the normal rounds of life, they need to be allowed and fully felt so that they can be released from the body. Rather than letting them build up like a balloon ready to pop, letting go of these emotions allows us to return to a state of equanimity so that we can be more calmly present with whomever or whatever situation is before us—so that we can once again engage the practice of love.

Summary

What is it that stands in the way of hearing the truth and discerning God's will? It is precisely the act of clinging to or identifying with anything at all as equal to who we are and any boasting that goes along with it.

> Thus says the Lord, "Let not a wise man boast of his wisdom, and let not the mighty man boast of his might, let not a rich man boast of his riches; but let him who boasts boast of this, that he understands and knows Me." ~ Jeremiah 9:23-24

What, then, is the alternative to clinging to or identifying with anything at all?

FIVE

The Ultimate Choice: Obey God or Chart Your Own Course

> "There are two kinds of people: those who say to God, 'Thy will be done,' and those to whom God says, 'all right, then, have it your way.' " [1]
>
> ~C.S. Lewis

A. Adam and Eve chose to disobey God.

Adam and Eve were born into this world with free will and the inclination to partake of the forbidden fruit—to choose a life that was not what God had in mind for them. Instead of listening to God's desire and acting on what they heard in obedient service, they chose to disobey God (the original sin) yielding to their desire to do what they wanted to do instead. By wanting to be as God, they made the ultimate choice to separate themselves from his influence. In paradise one moment and alienated from God the next—all by a single choice.

Adam and Eve got the "I want to steer my own boat" inclination out of dry dock and it has been traversing across the waters of the world ever since. Rather than being born as pure light or essence as the Eastern path espouses, or as innocent beings or our real selves as other teachings purport, we enter this world with the inclination to follow our own will, chart our own course and to be in control of every aspect of our lives outside the influence of God.

Our culture today is replete with those who believe that it's perfectly fine to do whatever you want to do as long as it doesn't harm anyone else. They carry the garden of Eden tendency forward by defining freedom as "being able to do whatever you want to do whenever you want to do it." If and when they take over the helm of their ship in such a controlling way, God becomes their competitor rather than the one to be faithfully obeyed as the revealer of eternal wisdom and truth.

> "Every man would like to be God, if it were possible; some few find it difficult to admit the impossibility." [2]
> ~Bertrand Russell, Philosopher

B. Our culture wholeheartedly supports charting our own course by relying on self-effort.

Our culture teaches us powerful tools of the mind to analyze and control the outside world through self-effort. Based on the belief that "If it's going to be, it's up to me", it encourages us to work hard to control, manipulate and master these tools in order to achieve our desired goals. "Just Do It!" is Nike's command for all of us if we want to be great at something, applauded and even paid well for doing so.

Eastern teachings (i.e., Buddhism, Hinduism, etc.), New Thought, Self-Help and New Age ideologies are all based on self-effort. Self-effort starts with you and ends with you. The initial goals, plans and the results or lack of results attained, rest entirely on your shoulders.

> "Nor do I understand who there can be more wonderful than myself." [3]
>
> ~ Walt Whitman

> "Oneself, indeed, is one's savior, for what other savior would there be? With oneself well controlled one obtains a savior difficult to find." [4]
>
> ~ Buddha

Self-effort is based on the principle of cause and effect. If I put forth the effort (the cause) then I should get the desired result (the effect). Self-effort implies that you first have a goal or desired result in mind and then employ some form of self-effort (i.e., a method, technique or process) to achieve the goal. Do this effort (the cause) long enough and you will eventually get the result you are looking for.

From the looks of things, it appears that self-effort works. Countless stories abound of individuals who have risen up from nothing, become Olympic champions or achieved wealth at a young age. "Keep your eye on the prize", "Focus on what you want and don't look back until you achieve it" and "You can be, do and have it all if you follow my recipe for success," are words coming forth from motivational speakers and self-help gurus around the globe. "Look at what I did," they proclaim. "Just follow my recipe for success and you can achieve what I did too!"

Books, magazines and motivational speeches are replete with steps and techniques to achieve desirable goals. Do these three steps, they promise, and you will lose weight, increase your income, be successful or attract the person of your dreams. Self-help teachers abound hoping that you will buy into their promise that three steps are all that's needed to get what you want.

Internet gurus are easy to be found these days promising that if you take their webinars, attend their workshops, read their books and sign up for personal consultations, that wealth, success, love and happiness will come as a result. They are ready to teach you their prescription for success for a reasonable price, appearing to offer good value for the money invested.

They are also very persuasive in their webinar presentations and are masters at closing the gap between what you want on one end and how what they offer will help you get what you want on the other end. They are, in other words, the solution to help you make the changes and achieve the goals you are desiring.

Have you climbed aboard any of these self-effort-alone trains? If so, which ones and how did it go?

C. The Jesus Path, on the other hand, also advocates taking action, but action issuing forth from one's personal relationship with Jesus.

On the Jesus Path, it's all about relationship. It's about recognizing that the chief act of the will is not effort, but consent to a personal God who forgives and forgets, loves unconditionally and is there as a steadfast rock and guide.

Whereas the self-effort alone paths put the individual first in an attempt to achieve some end like enlightenment or obtaining greater wealth or accomplishments, this relational path is about putting God first by doing your best to listen to the Spirit of truth and then responding with a serving heart over and over again. Self-effort is needed for sure, but the type of self-effort that has God initiating your next steps and then guiding and supporting you each step of the way.

D. Four fishermen chose to follow Jesus.

Unlike Adam and Eve and the rich man who chose not to obey God's request, four fishermen decided to leave their nets (i.e., their occupations) and accept Jesus' call to follow him. All were invited to follow and all were free to choose to accept or reject the invitation.

In the following scene, imagine that you are there as an unnamed observer aware of what each fisherman looks like, how each one is feeling and what is going on in the environment. Listen also to what Jesus is saying and how the fishermen respond to him.

> "Now as Jesus was walking by the Sea of Galilee, he saw two brothers, Simon who was called Peter, and Andrew his brother, casting a net into the sea; for they were fishermen. And he said to them, 'Follow Me, and I will make you fishers of men.' Immediately they left their nets and followed him. Going on from there he saw two other brothers, James the son of Zebedee, and John his brother, in the boat with Zebedee their father, mending their nets; and he called them. Immediately they left the boat and their father, and followed Him." [5]

Now imagine Peter getting together with Andrew, James and John shortly afterward and the following conversation that might well have ensued:

"Hey, listen, I don't know about you guys, but I've worked my entire life at this fishing gig and I'm having some real reservations about giving it up. I'm deeply drawn to follow Jesus, don't get me wrong, but I'm feeling torn inside. Like you guys, I've spent most of my adult life perfecting my schtick and it has been my consistent source of income for me and my family that whole time.

I mean, being a fisherman is who I am! It's what I do and how I make my living! It's my daily routine that I've grown accustomed to. It's also how others know and relate to me as well. Do any of you feel a bit conflicted as I do? And you, James and John, are you gonna just leave your father in the boat to take over the family business all by himself?! I betcha he's thrilled about that!

As I see it, if I just leave all of this and follow Jesus, I stand to lose my friends, my reputation in the community and likely one or perhaps all of my family members and relatives besides! And, most everyone I know will think I've lost my marbles! This is not a happy picture.

And one last thing. I have no idea what's gonna happen next! I mean, how are we gonna eat? How will we make ends meet? Where are we gonna live? Will we be protected when the heavy rains come in just a few months? How will we support our families while we're on the road? Will we come back and visit occasionally? All this uncertainty and having to trust Jesus that all will be taken care of somehow if we just follow him, has me more than a little freaked out. Are any of you feeling the same way?"

This imaginary but possible scenario points to the potent inclination we all have to:

- ~ Cling firmly to our hard-earned identity and the reputation that comes with it.
- ~ Be identified with our doubts, fears and attachments that keep us holding on for dear life to what is familiar, safe and secure.
- ~ Be reluctant to surrender our lives totally to God by consistently listening to him and following his lead.

E. God gives us the freedom to choose how we want to be.

One school of thought asserts that we are 100% conditioned or controlled by our past upbringing and religious and societal influences; that no one has free will. In contrast, Jesus says that we are free to choose.

From Adam and Eve on down, God has given us the freedom to go beyond our social conditioning and to choose between right and wrong, truth and falsity and good and bad. In the very details of our lives, he has given us free will to choose however we want to be. For example, while never forcing us to comply,

God gives us the freedom to be:

| Accepting | or | Critical |
| Empathetic | or | Hard-hearted |

God gives us the freedom to be (cont.):

Grateful	or	Ungrateful
Positive	or	Negative
Kind	or	Mean-spirited
Truthful	or	Dishonest
Open	or	Closed
Patient	or	Impatient
Purposeful	or	Aimless
Diligent	or	Apathetic
Responsible	or	Irresponsible
Courageous	or	Fearful
Temperate	or	Glutinous
Chaste	or	Lustful
Humble	or	Proud
Generous	or	Greedy
Other-centered	or	Self-centered

Aware of our true identity as children of God here to do our best to listen to and follow the Spirit of truth's guidance each step of the way and to use our personality and talents for the service of others and the glory of God.

or

Focused on building, fostering and preserving our fleeting identity and reputation based on what we do, what we have amassed and what we have achieved in order to be admired, validated and accepted by others and ourselves.

If we choose to follow the Spirit of truth, what are the avenues through which he speaks? The following chapter spells out what these avenues are so that we can grow in our ability to recognize his voice, respond to what we hear and thus grow in greater love of God and others.

SIX

The Art of Growing in Greater Love of God

> "Happy the one who listens to me, attending daily at my gates, . . ."
>
> ~ Proverbs 8:34

One primary way of growing in love of God is to consistently engage the practice of love. It is doing our best to listen to him, both in quiet times of prayerful reflection and throughout the day, and then to act on what we hear in a disposition of loving service. In order to listen to him, we need to be aware of the main channels through which he speaks.

A. To provide us with solid input from which to make God-guided decisions in matters big and small, the Spirit of truth speaks most commonly through:

1. People
2. Our body

3. Our gut or intuition
4. Common sense, conventional wisdom and important facts and information
5. Sacred Scripture and Church teaching
6. The experiences and details of everyday life

After communicating with us through one or more of these channels, the Spirit then joins us in the sanctuary of our conscience to help us sift through all of the input and arrive at decisions that feel right and true.

Conscience is the link between ourselves and God.

Taken from the church document, *Gaudium et Spes*, here is the clearest explanation I have found to date that explains how conscience is the main point of contact between ourselves and God:

> "In the depths of his conscience, man detects a law which he does not impose upon himself, but which holds him to obedience. Always summoning him to love good and avoid evil, the voice of conscience when necessary speaks to his heart: do this, shun that.
>
> For man has in his heart a law written by God; to obey it is the very dignity of man; according to it he will be judged. Conscience is the most secret core and sanctuary of a man. There he is alone with God, whose voice echoes in his depths. In a wonderful manner, conscience reveals that law which is fulfilled by love of God and neighbor.

In fidelity to conscience, Christians are joined with the rest of men in the search for truth, and for the genuine solution to the numerous problems which arise in the life of individuals from social relationships." [1]

It is there in the deep recesses of our conscience that:

~ God plants the seeds (i.e., laws) of right and wrong, good and evil and truth and falsity in us when we are born.

- No matter what our level of experience, education, economic status or social and religious upbringing happen to be, our conscience tells us that such things as killing, lying, cheating, stealing, coveting our neighbor's spouse and property, pornography, pedophilia, rape, incest, harmful addictions and drug, child and human trafficking are not right.
    In other words, we all have a law or moral compass inside of us that directs us to do good and avoid evil that, when followed, helps us grow in love of God, our neighbor and ourselves. We all have a conscience that directs us to do unto others as we would have them do unto us.

- Despite those political and social elites who proclaim in word and action that we the people have no right to conscience and that we must comply with all they tell us because they know what is best for us, we all have the God-given right and freedom to follow our conscience. Based on Judeo-Christian principles and the belief that God has given us free will, we all have the freedom to choose what is right, true and good.

~ We are alone with God each day listening for the kernels of truth that come to us through one or more of the avenues through which the Spirit of truth speaks.

~ We join with the Spirit of truth to help us sift out the wheat from the chaff; to recognize his voice over all other voices clamoring to be heard so that we can discern the truth and make God-guided choices.

Although God has spoken to us in the past through the prophets, saints, inspired writings and Jesus' own life and words, he is now in personal communication with each of us through our conscience that no individual, group or governmental body seeking to control can ever take away.

Few people recognize that discernment, or doing our best to listen to and follow God speaking through our conscience, lies at the heart of Christian spirituality.

While participating in church services, studying and meditating on Scripture, engaging various prayer forms and devotionals, tithing, and getting involved in church activities, classes and volunteering can definitely help us deepen our love of God and neighbor, they are not the essence of what it means to be a follower of Jesus.

The essence involves a personal and dynamic

relationship with God in which we consistently do our best to listen to him in the sanctuary of our conscience and then to act on what we hear in loving service. While some may have a greater capacity than others to discern his voice, all have the capacity nonetheless and can get better at it over time. Once again, the highest degree of peace possible on this planet is to be on the same page with God; to be in sync with his holy will.

B. Let us now consider the six most common avenues through which the Spirit of truth speaks:

1. The Spirit of truth speaks through people.

It is often the case that people who know us well and want what is best for us, are able to see us more clearly than we see ourselves. They are frequently able to observe and point out things that we may not be able to see. Whether they be our mate, friend, sibling, parent, teacher or pastor, these confidantes can help us identify the truth about the issue or question at hand and thus help us move closer to making good decisions.

If we are teachable and committed to hearing the truth, then listening closely to our spiritual friends or confidante(s) can be very helpful. On the other hand, if we do not consult our reliable confidantes, our discernment runs a much higher chance of being inaccurate.

That being said, our spiritual confidantes are not always right. That is why St. Paul recommends that we "Test everything and retain what is good."[2] On the other hand, if all our confidantes agree that we are not hearing the full truth about some aspect of our decision making, we would do well to step back and take more time before making a final decision.

The characteristics to look for in choosing a spiritual confidante

A spiritual confidante is someone who is there to help us make God-guided decisions by doing such things as:

- ~ Being fully and calmly present and listening well.
- ~ Challenging us to see if we are listening to our own ego, the call of the world around us or to our conscience.
- ~ Challenging us to go beyond merely doing whatever we want for selfish gains, relying too much on our head or heart or choosing from what we've done in the past.
- ~ Mirroring back to us what we are really communicating—"You seem frustrated, excited about, hesitant about, drawn to, etc."
- ~ Giving opinions sparingly, never telling us what they think we should do but asking questions instead in order to draw the truth out of us.

Is there anyone in your life who would make a good spiritual confidante?

2. The Spirit of truth speaks through our body.

For example, while swimming one morning, I felt an excruciating pain in my chest. I immediately stopped in my lane, clutched both hands over my heart and wondered if this was what a heart attack felt like. After a very long minute, the pain subsided and I slowly got out of the pool. Upon arriving home, I told my wife what had happened, but neither of us viewed the incident as an immediate cause for concern.

The next morning, after making my third trip upstairs, the piercing pain in my chest returned. Like the previous day, the pain lasted about a minute. Having never seen me in such pain before, Janie said, "You need to go to the emergency room, now!" I agreed.

After administering a battery of tests, the ER doctor sent me upstairs for a stress test. I lasted about 60 seconds on the treadmill before the wrenching pain appeared again. Once my heart rate returned to normal, the doctor explained the options to me in a calm and straightforward way.

That afternoon I had a heart catheterization done in which the doctor inserted a stent in an artery that turned out to be 80% clogged.

"The other arteries looked squeaky clean," he said. "Your working out regularly and eating well likely saved you from having a heart attack."

After staying in the hospital overnight for observation, I returned home the following day. In this instance, my body and my wife were definitely partners in discernment.

We live in a culture that largely ignores the body's wisdom.

While the signals that our bodies provide are not infallible, they often provide us with important input that can aid our discernment process.

For example,

A good decision is often accompanied by:	**A poor decision is often accompanied by:**
• Relaxed muscles • Slow and deep breathing • Released tension • Feelings of well-being	• Tight muscles, bodily pain • Shallow breathing • Bodily tension, headaches, stomach aches • Uneasy feelings

Since every body is different, we all need to become familiar with our own unique bodily clues and the wisdom they communicate.

3. The Spirit of truth speaks through our gut or intuition.

Not trusting the truth revealed through our gut and intuition can be quite costly in more ways than one. For example, several years ago, a writer friend of mine rented a booth at a street Book Fair on 5th Avenue in New York City. With books in hand, she set up her display and began greeting customers.

Her books were selling like hotcakes when a man in a green polo shirt, khaki pants and brown penny loafers approached her. After introducing himself as a very successful publicist backed by an impeccable brochure with a long list of accomplishments, he said, "Sarah, I can hit home runs for you!"

Having just talked with her husband that morning about wanting to get a publicist to take her books to the next level, they were excited about the prospects.

Their minds told them:	Voila! Here's the guy we've been waiting for!
Their gut and intuition told them:	This guy talks the big talk and sounds like he just came from a seminar entitled, "A Sucker Is Born Every Minute: How to Get Someone to Give You their Money Without Lifting a Finger."

Instead of waiting for him to come through with the goods before paying him any cash, a week later she mailed him a check for $7,500. For that payment, he landed her one radio interview. That's right, ONE interview! Little did she know that the next level would be one floor down—that his promised "home run" would turn out to be a foul ball.

Failing to trust her gut cost her a pretty penny. Failing to listen to her intuition again seventeen years later, cost her half of her life's savings. With hindsight being 20/20, she saw that the Spirit of truth was trying to get through via her gut reactions, but she did not listen.

Do you remember a time when you also did not listen to the Spirit of truth speaking through your gut or intuition which ended up costing you in more ways than one? On the other hand, do you remember times when you did follow your gut or intuition that yielded good fruit?

4. The Spirit of truth speaks through common sense, conventional wisdom and important facts and information.

My friend Mark was considering becoming a Future's trader. He said that a friend of his told him that he could make a lot of money doing this type of trading and that he would be glad to show him the ropes.

The conventional wisdom that he received from five people told him to drop this idea like a hot potato because it was far too risky. The facts were very clear that only 5% of those who did this type of trading were successful.

Common sense also chimed in revealing that he did not have any extra money to lose, that he would be putting his family at risk and that his personality temperament was not at all suited for this nerve-racking type of work.

Likewise, the information he received clearly warned against doing trading because it was gambling pure and simple and that he'd be running the risk of getting addicted to it just like any other form of gambling. In the end, he ignored all of this input and stubbornly held his ground believing that he would be part of the rarified 5%.

After joining the 95% club, losing a good deal of money and watching his heart literally pulsate through his shirt with each trade, it took him eight months before the addictive urge to trade finally went away.

In retrospect, he saw that the Spirit of truth was trying to get through to him at the time, but he was not open to letting that truth in. He realized that he was doing the work for the sole purpose of obtaining money, which is never a motivation that leads to a meaningful career, let alone to consistent financial rewards.

Do you remember a time or two when you also did not listen to the Spirit of truth speaking through your common sense, conventional wisdom and important facts and information? On the other hand, do you remember times when you did heed the truth revealed through these avenues that resulted in positive outcomes?

5. The Spirit of truth speaks through Sacred Scripture and church teaching.

> "Heaven and earth will pass away, but my words will never pass away."
> —Matthew 24: 35

God's word is eternal with the power to move, inspire and guide anyone who is open to it. Unlike everything else that we can see, hear, touch, taste and smell, God's word will not gradually change and pass away. It is there as a perpetual light guiding our steps and shining on the darkness that we encounter along the way. It is there as a holy teaching showing us how to grow in genuine love of God, others and ourselves.

As the Father lived on the inside of Jesus to the point of abiding in every part of his being, the more we immerse ourselves in the life and teachings of Jesus, the wisdom of the Old Testament and the scripture-based moral teachings and documents of the church, the more he will be in every part of our being helping us make more God-guided decisions.

Thus, it makes perfect sense to study and pray with the sacred scriptures and the scripture-based moral teachings and documents of the church in order to have a strong foundation from which to make good choices during the rounds of everyday life.

That being said, the scriptures and church teachings alone cannot possibly give us a full and complete list of all the rights and wrongs, goods and bads and truths and falsehoods that exist. There are many issues on which

Jesus was silent. For example, he did not speak about what your spouse or child needs right now, bio ethics, cloning or test tube babies or whether or not it's right or wrong to experiment with human genetics. The Church's teaching on these and other issues are based on the general principles derived from the sacred scriptures rather than from direct scripture passages themselves.

While the Bible offers tremendous wisdom and guidance on how to live a good, moral and loving life, most of the situations we find ourselves in and decisions we are confronted with each day, are not mentioned anywhere in the Bible. It is a guidebook for sure in which the Spirit of truth can and does speak to us through these inspired words, but not a moral decision-making playbook with all the plays and right decisions laid out ahead of time.

Likewise, the clergy, even those trained in spiritual direction, moral theology or ethics, cannot ever hope to completely inform our conscience so that we will know exactly what to do and say in every situation. Rather than attempting to provide us with ready-made answers and a detailed list of rights and wrongs as many have attempted to do in the past, they need to trust and affirm that:

- ~ God has planted the seeds of right and wrong, good and evil and truth and falsity in all of us when we are born.

- ~ We all have the capacity to discern God's voice and to get better at it over time.

- ~ Spiritual confidantes and spiritual directors are a great aid in helping us make well-considered, God-guided decisions.

Based on that trust, church leaders of the future would

do well to focus on helping us grow spiritually by doing all they can to aid our ability to recognize God's voice and will in the depths of our conscience and then to act on what we hear with a servant's heart. Is there anything more important than growing in our ability to discern God's wishes for us in matters big and small and then acting consistently on what we hear?

6. The Spirit of truth speaks through the experiences and details of everyday life.

> "It's a crazy world and life speeds by at a blur, yet God is right in the middle of the craziness. And anywhere, at any time, we may turn to Him, hear His voice, feel His hand, and catch the fragrance of heaven." [3]
> ~Joni Eareckson Tada

We can find God in all things because God is everywhere. No matter what situation or circumstance we are in or whom we are with, God is there. He is present as that still, small voice guiding and nudging us to **listen** to the truth of whatever is being communicated through a person, circumstance or topic at hand and then giving us the courage to **act** on what we hear.

For example, you may:

~ Be reading Sacred Scripture and have a personal insight jump out at you.

~ Be involved in a close relationship and suddenly realize the truth about why that person has been pulling away from you.

- Be listening to a podcast or reading a book and gain new understanding.

- Have a traumatic event occur in your life that turns out to be an unforeseen blessing moving you to make a positive change in your life.

- Be watching a movie and be moved to spend more quality time with your family like you saw an actor doing on the screen.

- Ask God a question before going to bed and receive an answer in the morning in the state between sleeping and waking.

Or,

- Relative to work, God may plant a strong desire in your heart to do something specific and then give you the courage to act boldly on that desire.

- As God has communicated to many in the Scriptures through dreams, you may receive a nudge or message in a dream or have a recurring dream that is calling you to pay attention to something in particular.

- You may also find God speaking to you via certain experiences that occur in your life.

C. Three Steps to Making a Thorough, God-Guided Decision

Step 1: **Formulate the right question.**

It is extremely important to formulate the right question. For example, you may initially come up with a question like: Should I take this particular job? However, if you delved into your situation more deeply, the more correct question might be: Should I stay home with my daughter at this important time before she heads off to college in six months?

Before examining your particular question more in detail, you need to honestly assess whether or not you are actually open to the truth of what is right and best for you. For instance, if you have any pre-set idea, prejudice, bias, partisanship or strong conviction about what you should or should not do, it needs to be recognized and cleared out before any true information gathering and decision-making process can take place.

Step 2: Gather all the Spirit of truth data you can.

After formulating the right question, next gather all the Spirit of truth data you can. This gathering is done by listening for the truth with open eyes, an open mind and a softened heart as revealed through the most common avenues through which the Spirit communicates.

After gathering all the Spirit of truth data you can, here is a simple sentence completion exercise to help you make a well-considered choice relative to the decision at hand:

1. My body tells me . . .

2. My gut or intuition tells me . . .

3. Common sense and conventional wisdom tell me . . .

4. Some important facts and background information are . . .

5. Sacred Scripture and/or church teaching tell me . . .

6. My experiences in everyday life tell me . . .

7. After consulting with my spiritual confidante(s), I get the sense that . . .

While no single piece of data is usually enough in itself, together they can help point you in the right direction.

Step 3: Pray about the data you've received.

After completing the sentence-completion exercise, then sit in prayer with your responses until you gradually live into an answer that feels right, true and good—that leaves you with an abiding sense of peace and joy.

D. How to tell when God is communicating versus your own ego or other influences

Discerning God's voice is not always easy to do. Most saints, spiritual directors and Christian writers over the centuries agree that you can never know for sure if it is God communicating, not this side of the grave anyway. However, they point to indicators of when you are most likely on the right track and when you are not when making a particular decision.

Here are some of those main indicators:

You are most likely on the right track (under the influence of the true Spirit)[4] when you:	You are most likely not on the right track (under the influence of the false spirit) when you:
Feel joyful and peaceful about your choice *over a good period of time.*[5]	Feel a gnawing anxiety and turmoil about your choice *over a good period of time.*
Are open and transparent and receive confirmation about your choice from at least 1-2 spiritual friends or confidantes who want you to follow God's lead.	Are closed off and secretive and do not include others in your decision making process believing that you can make the choice on your own.
Are focused outward in your energy and attention and are enthusiastic about your proposed choice.	Are pulled in on yourself and not looking forward to carrying out your proposed choice.
Feel courageous with a strong desire to carry out your proposed decision with your own unique creative expression.	Feel afraid and confused with a lack of clarity about your proposed decision.

Perhaps the closest you'll get to knowing if you've heard clearly is if the action you take as a result of your decision brings about what is called the fruit of the Spirit. The fruit of the Spirit is love, joy, peace, patience, kindness, generosity, faithfulness, gentleness, and self-control."[6]

If your activities in the world produce many or most of these virtues, then it is generally thought that you have heard clearly and responded well. In other words, when you make a particular choice and are more loving, joyful, peaceful, kind, generous, faithful, gentle and are exerting self-control after making that choice, it is generally thought that you have made a God-guided decision.

E. If your intention is to follow God and do what is right, you will eventually get it right.

> "If today you hear His voice, harden not your hearts."
>
> ~ Hebrews 3:7-8

Like a mother who can pick out her child's voice in a large crowd, over time we become better able to discern the voice of the Holy Spirit when it calls amidst an array of contrary voices competing to be heard.

Over time,

- ~ An intuitive sense of what is right shines forth amidst such opposing voices as fear, doubt, guilt, rebelliousness, reactivity and confusion.
- ~ A basic sense of truth can be heard over the shoulds echoing from our upbringing, societal customs, old belief systems and habitual ways of thinking.

Often we listen the best we can and then do what seems to be the right thing to do at the time. Sometimes, however, we make choices that are off the mark. No problem. We may have been given wrong information or failed to take key factors into consideration.

The **intention** to follow God and do what is right is what is important. If the good intention is there, we will eventually get it right, even if we make a few poor decisions along the way, which we most surely will.

The Road Ahead

The following quote from the late Trappist monk, Thomas Merton, illustrates that we often don't know if we are in sync with God's will, but that our intention to please him may well be what matters most:

> "My Lord God, I have no idea where I am going.
> I do not see the road ahead of me.
> I cannot know for certain where it will end.
> Nor do I really know myself, and the fact that I think I am following your will
> does not mean that I am actually doing so.
> But I believe that the desire to please you
> does in fact please you.
> And I hope I have that desire in all that I am doing.
> I hope that I will never do anything apart from that desire.
> And I know that if I do this you will lead me by the right road, though I may know nothing about it.
> Therefore will I trust you always though
> I may seem to be lost and in the shadow of death.
> I will not fear, for you are ever with me,

and you will never leave me to face my perils alone.
Amen." [7]

Summary

Our love for God can grow by consistently doing our best each day to:

- ~ Listen for his voice of truth that comes through all of creation and most clearly through people, our body, our gut or intuition, common sense, conventional wisdom, important facts and information, Sacred Scripture and Church teaching and the experiences and details of everyday life.

- ~ Join with the Spirit of truth in the sanctuary of our conscience to help us sift through any of the above input and arrive at decisions that feel right and true and leave us with an abiding sense of peace and joy.

- ~ Act consistently on what we hear in a disposition of loving service.

In addition to engaging the practice of love and doing such things as participating in church services, studying and meditating on Scripture, engaging various prayer forms and devotionals and getting involved in church activities, the following chapter offers seven ways of acting and praying that have helped many over the centuries deepen their love of God.

SEVEN

Seven Ways to Help Deepen Your Love of God

The more we learn about love, the more we learn about God.

#1: Love God by loving your neighbor.

> ". . . 'Truly I say to you, as you did it to one of the least of these My brothers, you have done it to Me.'"
>
> ~ Mt. 25:40

> ". . . for I was hungry, and you gave me food to eat. I was thirsty and you gave me something to drink, I was a stranger and you welcomed me, . . .
>
> ~ Mt. 25:35

We grow in love of God by consistently:

~ Acknowledging that the Father loves everyone and sends the sun and the rain on the good and the bad.

~ Loving everybody whether they be rich or poor, educated or uneducated, Christian or Muslim, Catholic or Protestant, Hindu or Buddhist, black or white, religionist or non-religionist, conservative or liberal and atheist or believer.

"Nothing we do is of value if there is not the feeling of love for our brothers and sisters in it."[1]

~ Chiara Lubich, founder of the Focolare movement

~ Putting others first and seeing the face of God in each person we meet.

~ Emptying ourselves daily of any preoccupying problems, concerns and judgments in order to be more fully and calmly present with those who cross our path.

~ Welcoming and blessing whoever is before us as they are with a willingness to learn from them.

~ Listening to the needs, wants, fears and frustrations of others and responding with a giving heart.

~ Taking on the sufferings of others as our own and thus helping to relieve some of their burdens. In the words of St. Paul:

"To the weak I became weak. I have become all things to all people so that I might by any means save some people."

~ I Cor. 9:22

- Being willing to literally die for others in imitation of Christ who laid down his life for us as the highest expression of sacrificial love.

- Taking on the joys of others as our own and thus helping to expand their joys even further.

#2: Contemplate the life of Jesus using your imagination. [2]

St. Ignatius of Loyola realized that one of the best ways of coming to know Jesus, feeling his deep love and receiving his guidance in daily life was to meditate on him in the Gospels while using our imagination. Being powerfully attracted to Jesus, Ignatius experienced first hand that these sacred writings were one of the key ways God has of communicating with us. Saints Basil, Augustine, Gregory the Great and Bede also wrote about this form of contemplation.

To provide others with a similar opportunity to know Jesus more personally, he developed a form of prayer called Imaginative Contemplation. This prayer, which he adapted from use in medieval monasteries, allowed beginners and those more experienced in prayer, to open their minds and hearts to experience the word of God as fully as possible.

In this prayer, the individual employs the five senses while contemplating the actions and words of Jesus. By so doing, the person sets the stage for knowing Jesus more intimately and developing a personal and unique relationship with him.

The Practice of Love

Here's how it works:

1. Choose a Gospel story (see the list below of 24 Gospel stories) and pray for the grace to know Jesus more personally and to be open to hearing what message or instruction he may have for you.

   Some stories from the Gospels of Matthew, Mark, Luke and John to meditate on while using Imaginative Contemplation are:

The birth of Jesus	Matt. 1:18-25
The temptation of Jesus	Matt. 4:1-11
The call of the first disciples	Matt. 4:18-22
The cleansing of the leper	Matt. 8:1-4
The healing of the paralytic	Matt. 9:1-8
The rich young man	Matt. 19:16-22
The call of Levi	Mark 2:13-17
Raising the daughter of Jairus	Mark 5:21-43
The calming of a storm at sea	Mark 5:35-41
Walking on the water	Mark 7:45-51
The transfiguration of Jesus	Mark 9:2-8
Blind Bartimaeus	Mark 10:46-52
Blessing the children	Luke 19:15-17
The call of Zacchaeus	Luke 19:1-10
The Last Supper	Luke 22:14-23
The agony in the garden	Luke 22:39-46
The crucifixion	Luke 23:33-49
Journey to Emmaus	Luke 24:13-35
The wedding at Cana	John 2:1-11
Cure of lame man at the pool	John 5:2-9

Miracle of the loaves	John 6:1-13
Walking on the water	John 6:16-21
Woman caught in adultery	John 8:2-11
Jesus and Peter	John 21:15-19

2. As you are reading the story, look at the overall scene and be aware of what you see, hear, feel and smell. Watch Jesus' face, listen to what he says and how the people respond to him. Notice what they look like, how each one is feeling and what is going on in the environment. You can imagine yourself as an unnamed person in the crowd, as a character in the story, or, in the case of the Gospels, as Jesus himself. At any point during the meditation, you can stop and converse with Jesus.

3. When you have finished, be still and simply enjoy being in the Lord's presence. Then, if you wish, record any thoughts, feelings and messages that came to you during the meditation or how it speaks to your current life situation.

#3: Meditate on the life and death of Jesus in a personal and intimate way by watching *The Chosen* and *The Passion of the Christ* and its sequel, *The Passion of the Christ: Resurrection*.

Directed and co-written by filmmaker Dallas Jenkins, *The Chosen* is the first multi-season series about the life and ministry of Jesus as seen through the eyes of people who encountered Him.

Produced, directed and co-written by Mel Gibson, *The Passion of the Christ* primarily covers the 12 hours before Jesus' death interspersed with moments in Jesus' life. Watch also its sequel, *The Passion of the Christ: Resurrection.*

Check the internet for ways to view these offerings on various devices.

#4: Have written dialogues with God.

> "Be still and know that I am God." [3]

> "God speaks in the silence of the heart. Listening is the beginning of prayer." [4]
> ~ St. Mother Teresa of Calcutta

If we do not take time to be still and pray in the lap of silence, all we have are to-do lists, responsibilities and a hectic pace of life—all we hear are noises and the constant chatter of the mind. If we do not listen regularly to the Spirit of truth and love in the unmovable center at the eye of the hurricane, we cannot help but be thrown off balance and gradually worn down by the thousands of thoughts, images, feelings and bodily sensations that capture our attention each day.

The following way of praying uses written dialogue as a vehicle for deepening our relationship with God:

- ~ To calm the body-mind, take a few deep breaths, letting go of all tension, anxiety and worry.
- ~ In your journal or notebook, write the date and your initials on the left side of

the paper. Next to your initials begin your conversation by expressing whatever is on your mind and heart. You can also ask a question that needs God's wisdom and guidance.

~ Next, write "G" for God, "L" for Lord or "J" for Jesus and write down what he says back to you. The important thing is to just let the words flow out smoothly without worrying if you are putting words in his mouth or not. Once he is done speaking, then respond by saying whatever else comes to mind. Trust that whatever truth, message or outcome that needs to come forth will be revealed in the course of the dialogue. Stay with the conversation going back and forth until it naturally comes to an end.

~ When you have finished dialoguing, be still and simply enjoy being in God's presence. If you wish, record any insights, feelings or guidance that came to you during the conversation.

#5: Be grateful for everyday blessings.

"In all circumstances give thanks for this is the will of God for you in Christ Jesus." [5]

Believing that God is present in all of his creation and the origin of and revealer of all truth, we approach each day and all that it might contain as coming from God. Noticing that everything we can see, hear, touch, taste and smell is a graceful gift of God revealing his loving and creative

The Practice of Love

presence, we engage the practice of thanking him often during the day for the various people, things, events and circumstances that come our way and any truths that may accompany them.

The Prayer of Gratitude for Everyday Blessings can be expressed in such ways as:

- ~ Saying "thank you, Lord" for such things as a parking place, the blue sky, rain, a text, a happy dog wagging his tail, billowy clouds, a gentle breeze, green trees, rolling green hills, a phone call, the warm sun, a hug or someone sharing their story with you.

- ~ Being grateful for what you have rather than focusing on what you don't have.

- ~ Giving thanks for things you normally take for granted like food, water, shelter, clothing, simple pleasures, a loving family, friends, a good education, a good job, your cell phone, your computer, the money that allows you to sustain yourself and for the ability to come up with your day's priorities.

- ~ Welcoming others with a smile, saying thank you, writing thank you notes, praising people and simply being grateful for who is in your life right now.

- ~ Keeping a gratitude journal.

- ~ Saying a prayer of gratitude to God for all that he has done for you.

"Let your lives overflow with thanksgiving for all he has done." [6]

~ Saying a prayer of gratitude for all those in your life who have helped you grow in greater love of God, others and yourself.

~ Thanking God for the lessons you have learned from all the difficulties, challenges and relationships you have had, realizing that they were actually blessings in disguise.

If you tend to:

- See the glass as half-empty
- Be critical of yourself and others
- Have trouble accepting your present reality as it is
- Be crabby and pessimistic
- Focus on what you haven't gotten done or what you don't have
- Be anxious and worry a lot,

being grateful can go a long way in helping you reduce these tendencies and live a more positive and happy life.

#6: Be aware of God's presence in the ordinary and pleasurable activities of life and converse with him throughout the day.

"God can be found in everyone, in every place and in everything." [7]

~St. Ignatius of Loyola

The Practice of Love

Brother Lawrence, a Carmelite brother, found the presence of God while doing such mundane things as cooking, washing dishes and sweeping the floor. In the noise and clatter of the kitchen, he saw it all as a time for prayer and conversing with God.

> "It is not necessary to have great things to do. I turn my little omelet in the pan for the love of God." [8]

Brother Lawrence's life reminds us to be aware of God's love and presence during all the repetitive chores, activities and pleasures of life. Whether we are:

> Taking a shower
> Preparing for the day
> Making a meal
> Eating something
> Working out
> Shopping
> Sitting in a parked car
> Taking a walk
> Standing in line
> Working a job
> Taking a bathroom break
> Running errands
> Talking on the phone
> Sending a text
> Reading Sacred Scripture
> Driving
> Enjoying a favorite hobby,
>
> it is there in the ordinary that we recognize God's presence and converse with him.

Finding God in Pleasurable Activities

> "God wants us to have joy in our souls and health in our bodies." [9]
>
> ~ Hildegard of Bingen

Many people assume that if you are having fun or enjoying some pleasurable activity, there must be something wrong with it. They may unconsciously believe that they must first complete all their work, pay off all their bills or that pleasure must be earned before they can have a moment of enjoyment. However, since God gives us the world to live in and enjoy, pleasure is actually a place to meet God.

Whether it be the pleasure of:

>Being in nature
>Eating
>Playing
>Hugging a loved one or pet
>Making love
>Watching a good movie
>Reading something
>Viewing art
>Enjoying a beautiful sunset or painting
>Singing
>Listening to our favorite music
>Knowing that we are loved by God and needed by him to carry on his healing message,
>
>all of these bring joy and help us be more fully alive.

The Practice of Love

Exercise:
In your mind, journal or notebook complete these phrases:

Most of my life I have tended to view pleasure as . . .

The times I did do pleasurable things, I usually felt . . .

If I began viewing pleasure as something endorsed by God and a way of encountering him, my life would . . .

The top three things I enjoy doing are . . .

Sitting in stillness, what pleasure would you like to enjoy soon and which one later on?

#7: Find God's peace in prayer by praying with millions on hallow.com, the #1 prayer app in the world.

Hallow is a prayer and meditation app for Christians everywhere to grow deeper in their relationship with God. It gives you the opportunity to experiment with different forms of prayer so that you can find the ones that most help you deepen your love of God.

EIGHT

The Art of Growing in Greater Love of Yourself

How we develop a level of self-love that is lower than we'd like.

The truth is that we have all said and done things in the past that we regret and that can make us feel bad about ourselves whenever we dwell on them. In addition, others have also said and done things that have hurt us deeply in one way or another that make it even easier to conclude that we are not acceptable and lovable as we are.

For example, we may have been:

>Neglected
>Rejected, betrayed, used or abandoned
>Physically, sexually or emotionally abused
>Criticized
>Bullied
>Smothered
>Unappreciated

Or experienced:

> Poor parenting
> Parents separating or divorcing
> Being placed in a foster home or orphanage
> Substance abuse by one or both parents
> The death of a family member
> Financial loss
> Illness, personal injury or major surgery
> A physical or learning disability
> Being unsuccessful in school, relationships or work
> Any combination of the above

From one or more of these experiences, we may have come to believe such false ideas as we are not good enough or that we are UN-intelligent, UN-attractive, UN-worthy, UN-creative, UN-successful, UN-likable, UN-lovable, Un-responsible or UN-acceptable as we are. As a result, we may have developed a level of self-love that is lower than we'd like.

With 0% being the lowest and 100% being the highest, where do you fall on the Self-Love Scale?

Self-Love Scale

0%............................50%............................100%
Low   High

Why is it essential to grow in genuine self-love?

If we do not love ourselves, then we cannot give to others and God what we don't have (i.e., love). If we are constantly wagging our inner index finger at ourselves, we cannot help but do the same thing in all of our relationships and thus unconsciously push others away, especially those we care about the most.

In short, if we choose to continue on with a lack of self-love (and it is a choice), we will be left with the direst of consequences—the inability to love anyone intimately.

The good news is that:

1. Your present level of self-love is NOT set in stone.

2. Unlike your IQ (Intelligence Quotient), which becomes stable around the age of 17, your level of self-love can and will increase gradually over time but only with your participation.

3. You can maintain a consistently high level of self-love the rest of your life.

Six ways to help you grow in genuine self-love:

Exercise:
As you read over these six ways in the pages that follow, write down any of the self-love enhancing actions that you may want to take on in the near future. Be sure to include any other actions that are not mentioned here. Later, you can choose to take on any of these actions one or two at a time per 60 day period knowing that you can only grow incrementally in genuine self-love and not in one fell swoop.

1. Embrace your past and learn from it rather than accept it as a life-sentence.

> "Those who do not learn from their past are destined to repeat it."[1]
>
> ~ George Santayana, Philosopher, Writer

Rather than bemoaning your past as the reason for your present unhappiness and lack of success in such things as relationships and work, it is helpful to:

- ~ View your past as a school to be learned from rather than as the cause of your present state of mind and heart. You are not the victim even though it is tempting to want to blame others or events for your unhappiness.

- ~ Remember that others will inevitably want to define you by your past and put you in a steel box. The real you is not who you were or what you did in the past.

- ~ Understand that all the apparently positive and adverse experiences, events and encounters up to this point in your life have helped make you into the person you are today—that you are where you are today because of your life experiences, not in spite of them.

- ~ Identify any experience, event or encounter from your past that still has a hold on you in the present, and then allow yourself to feel and release any residual feelings of anger, guilt, shame and anxiety that may have been trapped in your body for decades. Trust that when you allow yourself to feel, you heal.

~ Recognize whenever you start beating yourself up with negative self-talk about what you did or failed to do in the past, and then let it go through a few strong exhaled breaths.

~ Stop judging yourself from a standard of perfection or jumping to the conclusion that you are somehow bad or incapable whenever you have one negative experience. For instance, getting a bad grade on a biology test does not mean that you are therefore bad in science, an overall bad student or a bad person. Likewise, having difficulty in one or two relationships does not mean that you are incapable of ever having a happy and lifelong committed relationship.

~ Forgive yourself completely and accept God's forgiveness for what you have done or failed to do. Realize the absolute fact that you could not have made different decisions in the past because either you did not know any better at the time or lacked the information, insight and wisdom needed to choose differently.

While reading books, listening to podcasts, going to counseling or attending regular group meetings can be very helpful in gaining personal insight, working through your feelings and uncovering negative habit patterns, the point is to learn what you need to learn about your past, make the needed changes of thought and action and move on.

2. Consistently engage the practice of love.

The main antidote for a low level of self-love is to consistently engage the practice of love.

While not discounting for a moment the negative effect that poor parenting, traumatic events and negative experiences from your past might have had on you and the importance of getting good counseling and group support along the way, you have the choice each day to love or not to love. No matter how tired, stressed, sick, in pain or hungry you are at any given time, you are free to choose to enter into the sufferings and joys of others and be fully present to them or to do the opposite.

The truth is that whenever you do your best to listen to God for what is right and true and then act on what you hear in service of God and others, you feel genuinely good about yourself. Each time you move from self-preoccupation to listening with the ear of the heart to the needs, wants, fears and frustrations of others and responding in a caring and compassionate way, your level of self-love grows.

3. Let go of trying to please or control others to make you feel okay.

Millions of people are unconsciously dependent on and look solely to others in order to feel accepted, validated and loved. In their search for love outside of themselves, they are hyper-sensitive to such things as what others say to them, how others look at them, their tone of voice and what they are conveying through their body language. Their "Do they love me or love me not?" antennas are fully extended assessing everyone who crosses their path with a thumbs up or thumbs down depending on how they respond to them.

When others are upbeat, affirming and receptive, for instance, they feel good. On the other hand, when they are cranky, self-absorbed or unresponsive in some way, they feel bad. By depending on others to provide them with the feeling that they are okay, they tend to take things personally and feel offended when others do not pay attention to them, criticize them or fail to give them whatever "hit of positivity" they are looking for.

These seekers for love from others generally fall into two groups. While you can be a member of both groups, you generally fall more predominantly into one group.

Group 1 is the pleasing group. Members of this group tend to:

- ~ Defer to what others want and need without being aware of and expressing their own wants and needs.

- ~ Dance around the truth, be wishy-washy and play both sides of a situation and say "yes" when they mean "no" just to gain approval.

- ~ Worry about what others are thinking of them and want to make everyone happy and to like them in order to feel accepted.

The reality is that:

- ~ Most people are not thinking about you at all but are primarily concerned about what you and others are thinking of them!

- ~ You can't please everyone, no matter how hard you try. It is estimated that 25% of people are going to like you, 25% are not going to like you and 50% of people could go either way.

- ~ Since not everyone is going to like you, the only sane option is to be yourself and be friends only with those who accept, respect and appreciate who you are and will walk by your side no matter what.

- ~ When you consciously choose to engage the practice of love with everyone you meet, good people who genuinely appreciate and celebrate you will come into your life.

Group 2 is the controlling group. Members of this group tend to:

- ~ Be strongly identified with certain beliefs and actions and seek to feel loved by trying to control others to think, feel and act like they do.

- ~ Have rules for just about everything and feel loved when others obey their rules and unloved and unrespected when they do not.

To illustrate, after being diagnosed that he was gluten intolerant and that sugar was very harmful for him akin to throwing gasoline on the fire of inflammation, Bill held the belief that everyone, especially his wife and kids, should also avoid eating gluten and sugar.

Referencing such books as *Wheat Belly*, *Grain Brain* and *Sugar Blues*, he gave them what he considered to be logical facts about why gluten and sugar should be avoided. He explained how eliminating these two substances would not only aid digestion, but also help reduce brain fog, keep weight down and decrease inflammation in the body.

After recognizing that he identified with these rules as part of who he was and thus felt personally unloved and disrespected when they did not follow his advice, he was faced with two options:

1. To continue holding on to his rules and reacting angrily and feeling unloved every time he saw them ingesting these substances.

2. To apply these rules to himself alone.

Although he did choose option two, it did *not* mean that his tendency to control in this way suddenly vanished. In his own words, "When I catch myself about to react, I immediately take a few deep breaths instead of casting my judgmental stare or saying something I'll regret later. When I don't catch myself in time and react anyway, I simply apologize and move on."

Thus, from your experience, do you think it is possible to grow in genuine self-love by seeking to feel accepted, validated and loved by others or by trying to please or control others to make you feel okay?

While the authentic love of others does provide a solid base from which to grow in genuine self-love, others can never give us the fullness of love we are looking for. They can never satisfy our hungry hearts. When St. Augustine wrote, "Our hearts will not rest until they rest in Thee", he was echoing the truth that we will never experience the fullness of love we are yearning for until we cross the threshold of death and come to rest in the unconditional love and presence of God. In his own words:

> "When I am completely united to you,
> there will be no more sorrow or trials;
> entirely full of you, my life will be complete."[2]

4. See yourself as God sees you.

Holding on to a low self-image is like being locked in a prison cell with no chance of parole. One way out is to begin seeing yourself as God sees you. And how does God see you? Jesus reveals the answer in his story about the prodigal son:

> Then he said, "There was a man who had two sons. The younger one said to his father, 'Father, let me have the share of the estate that will come to me.' So the father divided the property between them.
> A few days later, the younger son got together everything he had and left for a distant country where he squandered his money on a life of debauchery. When he had spent it all, that country experienced a severe famine, and now he began to feel the pinch; so he hired himself out to one of

the local inhabitants who put him on his farm to feed the pigs. And he would willingly have filled himself with the husks the pigs were eating but no one would let him have them.

Then he came to his senses and said, "How many of my father's hired men have all the food they want and more, and here am I dying of hunger! I will leave this place and go to my father and say: Father, I have sinned against heaven and against you; I no longer deserve to be called your son; treat me as one of your hired men."

So he left the place and went back to his father. While he was still a long way off, his father saw him and was moved with pity. He ran to the boy, clasped him in his arms and kissed him.

Then his son said, "Father, I have sinned against heaven and against you. I no longer deserve to be called your son."

But the father said to his servants, "Quick! Bring out the best robe and put it on him; put a ring on his finger and sandals on his feet. Bring the calf we have been fattening, and kill it; we will celebrate by having a feast, because this son of mine was dead and has come back to life; he was lost and is found." And they began to celebrate.

~ Luke 15:11-24

Having lost his entire inheritance on a life of debauchery, he felt undeserving and unworthy to be called his father's son. For what he had done, he wanted to pay for his sin the rest of his life by being treated as one of his father's hired men.

While his brother was angry at his father because he had never thrown a party for him after being such a faithful servant all those years, the father took pity on his prodigal son, ran to him, put his best robe on him and gave him a hug and kiss. Rather than criticizing him for swallowing up his inheritance and galavanting with loose women, he rejoiced at his son's return by giving him a ring and sandals, killing a fattened calf and throwing a celebration.

How does this story show how God sees everyone? Based on this story and Jesus' life and teaching, here is a soliloquy that I imagine God would say to explain how he looks upon us:

> "I love *everyone* from babies in the womb to old folks inching toward the tomb. My love is so great, in fact, that I do not focus on your sin but only on who you really are and who you are becoming. I do not care about who you once were, but only about all the good you can and will do for me and others in this world.
>
> I see you as my child, my beloved creation with a unique DNA minus all the negative beliefs, feelings and internal chatter that you have going on inside your head. I even call you by name, not your birth name, but the name that incapsulates who you really are and what gives ultimate meaning and

purpose to your life.

Please do not spend one moment focusing on your sins nor falsely believing that you have committed the one unforgivable sin that deserves a lifetime of punishment. I want you to know that feeling bad about yourself and perpetually guilty is a complete waste of your valuable time and talents and a total lie that the devil wants you to swallow hook, line and sinker.

Instead, let yourself off the hook immediately and be set free from all negative self-judgment. Realize that you are simply human, fall short in the loving category everyday and thus are in need of my daily mercy and forgiveness. Yes, repent and confess the ways that you have used or hurt others and, if possible, ask for forgiveness from those you have hurt the most.

My job is always to welcome you back with open arms and get you back on track. When your attention starts going inward with negative self-condemnation, I am there to remind you to stop hanging your head and slouching your shoulders and to stand up straight, let go of your guilt and victim status and keep moving forward.

I do that because *I desperately need you* to be my eyes, ears and body in the world. I want and need you to take responsibility for what you can change, to accept what you cannot change and to use your unique personality and talents in fulfillment of the desire to serve that I have planted in your heart.

I also want you to realize that *all* of my past and present spokespersons have fallen short just like you have. It is you and all of these other wounded ones that I have chosen to spread my message.

Thus, all I ask is that you do your best to listen to me daily in prayer and throughout the day for what is right and true and then boldly act on what you hear with steadfast faith and courage.

Take one step at a time knowing that my grace is there with each step you take. You don't have to have everything completely mapped out ahead of time. Just take the next step and I will guide you to the next step and then the next. Just follow my lead and I will take care of the results and give you the people and the financial and spiritual sustenance you need."

5. Discover what gives ultimate meaning and purpose to your life.

Rather than wandering aimlessly through life with little or no zest or passion for anything or anyone, discovering what provides ultimate meaning and purpose to your life will:

- ~ Give you a clear sense of direction and a firm *why* behind everything you do.
- ~ Propel you to hit the ground running each day with genuine joy and enthusiasm.
- ~ Help you feel genuinely good about yourself whenever you work towards fulfilling your purpose.

In his seminal book, *Man's Search for Meaning*[3], Victor Frankl writes about his experience of being in the German concentration camp at Auschwitz and what kept people inspired to keep on living despite experiencing tremendous hunger and all the mental, emotional and physical torture that went along with life at the camp. He examines why some people gave up hope and died and why others survived.

Why did some give up hope and die in the concentration camp at Auschwitz?

According to Frankl, they had very little or nothing to live *for*. They were not able to identify anyone or anything that gave their life meaning and purpose.

For example, there was no one person or group of persons for whom they wanted to stay alive—no spouse, mate, family or God that motivated them to want to live on. Also, there were no goals, work projects or spiritual motivations that gave them the impetus to keep going.

When Frankl would ask these people what was most important and valuable in their lives, they literally could not come up with anything. All they could focus on was what was right in the front of them—the stench of bodies being burned, the desperate cries, the mental images of loved ones already having been murdered and a total lack of hope of ever coming out alive. They saw, touched, smelled, heard and tasted only that which they desperately wanted to escape.

Why did others survive?

Frankl said that the survivors all had one thing in common. They had someone or something to live *for* that was very meaningful and important to them. Some had a relationship or relationships that meant the world to them; others had a creative work that they felt passionate about and wanted to complete. Others had both.

They stayed alive by doing such things as fantasizing about their work and how it would be created and disseminated. They would go over the details of their project in their minds, see the finished product and feel the joy and help that it would bring to others. Whether it was relationships or a creative work that spurred them on, or a combination of both, they had something meaningful in their lives that caused them to want to live.

Over against the most horrible atrocities and conditions of the camp, what was most valuable, meaningful and important stood out for them like the sun shining through the darkest of clouds. Knowing their *why* empowered them to endure tremendous hardship.

Recognizing the preciousness of life like never before, they knew that if they were given a second chance at freedom, they would really make it count. Some did and some did not, of course, while some died of disease, starvation or other physical maladies. However, many ended up loving big, working big and creating big while deeply valuing their relationships and the freedom to do what they felt genuinely moved or called to do.

The Difference Between a Man-Centered and a God-Centered Purpose

A Man-Centered purpose of life revolves around such things as:

- ~ Acquiring and accumulating such passing things as identities, knowledge, fame, a good reputation, fortune, friends, pleasurable experiences and possessions.

- ~ Achieving your dreams relative to what you want to be, do and have.

- ~ Getting your basic and higher needs met.

- ~ Becoming fulfilled or healed as a personality, improving your personality, having the most balanced, strong or healthy body, possessing the most money and power, winning and completing the most goals.

- ~ Having the widest variety of experiences, traveling to the most places, living in desirable locations, being the most comfortable and secure or working yourself to the bone and then enjoying the fruits of your labor.

- ~ Engaging meditative and self-transcending practices on the Eastern path in order to become enlightened in which the individual self or ego is totally dissolved in the universal light.

A God-Centered purpose of life revolves around:

- ~ Loving God first by doing your best to listen to him and follow his guidance each step of the way.

- ~ Responding by putting others first and utilizing your God-given personality and talents for the service of others and the glory of God.

- ~ Surrendering to who God has created you to be and what he wants you to do.

- ~ Doing all of the above so that you might one day live with God and the saints forever in heaven.

6. Identify positive changes you want to make in the key areas of your life and then take responsibility for them one action at a time.

The bottom line is this: Anytime you listen for the truth relative to such things as your body, emotions, relationships, what you focus on, money and work and then take consistent responsibility for any of those areas, you grow in genuine self-love.

The more you grow in genuine self-love by taking consistent responsibility for the truth relative to the key areas of your life, the stronger you become as an individual and the more love you have to give in your relationships.

The more response-able you are, the more maturity and integrity you bring to the table which greatly increases your chances of having stable and happy relationships. The more you listen for the truth and act on what you hear in a disposition of loving service, the happier you become.

Exercise:
Below is a non-exhaustive list of actions that individuals have taken responsibility for in six key areas of their lives allowing them to deepen their level of self-love. As you read the following courses of action, consider making a list of any actions you might want to take up now or in the near future, and add any others to the list that come to mind.

Since it generally takes around sixty days for a new positive life action to take hold and become a habit, it is recommended that you choose no more than two such actions per sixty day period. When taking on a new habit, you need to accept the fact that you will not do it perfectly from start to finish. Thus, whenever your old habit creeps back in at times, "Cut yourself some slack and get back on track!"

A. After listening for the truth relative to your BODY, you grow in genuine self-love whenever you take consistent responsibility for such things as:

- ~ Working out.

- ~ Eating healthy food, taking needed supplements and drinking lots of water.

- ~ Being deliberately positive and other-serving versus being crabby whenever you are either tired, hungry, stressed, in pain, not feeling well or have overloaded intestines.

~ Giving up a bad habit or an addiction (i.e., alcohol, drugs, tobacco, sugar, working too much, being critical, electronic screens, sexing, pornography, gambling, etc.).

~ Getting the proper amount and quality of sleep you need.

~ Deliberately standing, moving and gesturing in a confident way.

~ Taking deep breaths throughout the day to calm the body-mind and be more fully present.

B. After listening for the truth relative to your EMOTIONS, you grow in genuine self-love whenever you take consistent responsibility for such things as:

~ Being able to say what you are feeling and wanting versus keeping quiet and expecting others to know what you are feeling and desiring.

~ Being aware of another's feelings and managing your responses to them like acknowledging that the person is angry and then choosing to listen and find out why they are angry instead of reacting in kind.

~ Allowing your feelings to be felt and managing your responses to them like feeling afraid and still doing what you need to do anyway.

~ Being vulnerable by listening empathetically to another's feelings without trying to solve or fix the problem associated with those feelings.

~ Accepting people and situations as they are and making the most of it versus complaining when people or situations are not as you would like them to be.

~ Exerting self-control over your impulses relative to money, food and sex.

~ Having preferences (what you'd prefer to happen) versus expectations which cause you to feel upset whenever expectations are not met.

C. After listening for the truth relative to your RELATIONSHIPS, you grow in genuine self-love whenever you take consistent responsibility for such things as:

~ Welcoming and connecting with people where they are and providing an expanded space of openness for them to speak freely and be themselves free of judgment.

~ Listening attentively to the needs, wants, fears and frustrations of others and responding with helpful words and deeds or simply being there for them.

- Surrounding yourself with positive people of high integrity who, by their example, naturally encourage you to be the real you and pursue your calling or heart's desire.

- Cultivating friendships only with people you like, trust and respect.

- Letting go of worn-out relationships that no longer serve you well.

- Treating strangers as friends you have yet to meet.

- Apologizing whenever you say or do things that are less than loving.

D. After listening for the truth relative to WHAT YOU FOCUS ON, you grow in genuine self-love whenever you take consistent responsibility for focusing on such positive and relationship-building things as:

What you have and thanking God often for your many blessings and for the lessons you have learned from all the difficulties and challenges you have had.	vs.	**What you don't have** or what is missing (i.e., I don't have my debts paid off or the right mate, living situation or job. I don't have enough money, experience, talent, skills, creativity, self-confidence, etc.)
Accepting and appreciating others as they are.	vs.	**What others don't have** or what is missing in their lives.

What you can control.	vs.	**What you can't control** (i.e., which is close to just about everything).
What the Spirit of truth is moving you to do or say in the present moment that is right, true and good.	vs.	**Negative memories, thoughts and feelings from your near or distant past,** causing you to feel bad.
Acting on the truth that you hear in service of others.	vs.	**Resisting the truth** while focusing primarily on your own wants, needs, fears and frustrations.

You become what you focus on.

For example, if you focus on any of the things in the right hand column above, you will become more negative and feel such things as stressed, depressed, miserable, frustrated, discouraged, sad or any combination thereof. As a result, when you become any of these negative feelings, others will not enjoy being around you.

On the other hand, if you focus on any of the things in the left-hand column above, you will become more positive, feel an abiding sense of peace and joy and others will enjoy your company.

What you focus on is all that you will tend to see.

If you focus on being a victim, for instance, then what you will tend to see and look for in your life is being victimized

The Practice of Love

by others. In one situation after another, you will unconsciously set it up so that you will once again be the victim and have yet someone else to blame.

Likewise, what you focus on tends to increase in size and intensity. For example, if you focus on what you don't like about someone else, then that focus will increase in size and magnitude until it becomes so BIG as to obscure any good qualities the other might have.

One sane alternative is to focus on what you appreciate about the other by zeroing in on the good they have done, are presently doing and will do in the future. Through this precise focus, you give gratitude, rather than negative judgment, the opportunity to increase in size and intensity.

Want to feel better and have happier relationships?

If you want to feel better and have happier relationships, then you have to take responsibility for where you focus your attention. Rather than letting your power of concentration go wherever it wants to go, as if it was somehow out of your control, you have the choice to harness it by focusing consistently on what you have, what you can control and on what the Spirit of truth is calling you to do in the present moment.

E. After listening for the truth relative to your MONEY[4], you grow in genuine self-love whenever you take consistent responsibility for such things as:

~ Tithing and investing 10% or more of your gross income every month.

- Paying off debts until you become debt-free.
- Having an emergency fund that covers 3-6 months of basic living expenses.
- Making and sticking to a budget.
- Only buying things you can pay cash for vs. spending money you don't have.
- Making sure you have a diversified investment portfolio rather than putting all your eggs in one or two baskets.
- Making all key financial decisions as a team (i.e., with your partner).

F. After listening for the truth relative to your WORK, you grow in genuine self-love whenever you take consistent responsibility for such things as:

- Discerning the work you most need to do and the world most needs to have done and then listening to and following God's lead each step of the way.
- Being organized and tackling the most important priorities of the day first aligned with the saying: "First things first; the rest is easy."
- Building key business relationships only with people you like, trust and respect.
- Moving through "no" answers, disinterest and criticism when promoting your

product or service knowing that not everyone wants or needs what you have to offer, and being ready and confident for the next promotional effort at hand.

~ Doing what you say you are going to do and on time, following through on clients' requests and returning phone calls, emails and texts in a timely manner.

~ Being early for work, meetings and appointments.

~ Being open to suggestions when what you are doing is not working.

Summary

Growing in greater love of yourself happens gradually whenever you listen to God for the truth and then take responsibility for such things as:

~ Learning from your past, making the needed changes and moving on.

~ Becoming aware of negative self-talk whenever it arises, letting it go through strong exhaled breaths and returning to being more fully present with whatever relationship, situation or task is at hand.

~ Becoming aware of whenever you are trying to please or control others in order to feel loved and then doing the opposite.

~ Discovering what gives meaning and

purpose to your life so that you have a clear sense of direction and a firm *why* behind all that you do.

~ Seeing yourself as God sees you —> as a fully forgiven and loved child of God here to listen to him and follow his lead by using your God-given personality and talents for the service of others.

~ Your body, emotions, relationships, what you focus on, money and work.

The more you take consistent responsibility, the more:

~ You will grow in genuine self-love.

~ Love you will have to give in your relationships.

~ Maturity you will bring to the table which greatly increases your chances of having healthy and happy relationships.

On the other hand, *not* taking responsibility will not only lower your level of self-love but will also negatively impact your relationships.

For example, if you choose to do such things as:

Eat poorly
Not exercise
Maintain one or more addictions
Let your reactive emotions of fear, sorrow or anger run the show

> Fail to listen well and communicate openly and honestly
> Be closed off to seeing the truth about yourself, your relationship(s), situations or the topic at hand
>
> Not take responsibility for your money (the #1 cause of relationship problems and breakups)
> Focus mostly on the negative in yourself, others and the world
> Fail to accept what is and make the most of it
>
> Fail to discover what gives meaning and purpose to your life so that you have little or nothing to live for
> Do a work you dislike that does not allow you to use your God-given personality and talents in service of others,
>
> your level of self-love will go down and your relationships will suffer the negative side effects right along with it. As you know, your choices not only affect you, but everyone around you as well.

That being said, if you are considering getting married, be sure to take responsibility for your past and each of these key areas in your life *before* walking down the aisle. If you do not, your past and irresponsible areas will eventually rear their heads and cause difficulties in your marriage—guaranteed!

If you are already married, in a committed relationship or single, it's never too late to begin taking responsibility for your past and any particular areas in your life that need attention. You, your partner, future mate and friends will be glad you did.

Very few couples ask the question, "What is the purpose of marriage?" In the context of this book, the purpose of a married relationship is to help each other get to heaven. And how do you go about doing that? By helping each other discern and follow God's wishes by listening daily with the ear of the heart and then by encouraging one another to act on what is heard with courage, consistency and a servant's heart.

The practice of love happens more easily with those we love, agree with and have a high degree of commonality. However, there are others with whom we disagree, dislike or have little in common. These are people who may have done or said something that left scars or hurt someone close to us.

Whoever these persons happen to be, the mere thought of them makes us feel such things as anger, bitterness and resentment. We wish that they could somehow change not only for their own betterment but to make us feel better as well.

The following chapter entitled, "Loving Your Enemies", helps us identify who our enemies are and offers options for how to go about loving and forgiving those whom we find difficult to love.

NINE

Loving Your Enemies

Jesus said some radical and countercultural things in his day, but perhaps none more challenging than his call to love your enemies.

Loving your enemies is not easy and does not happen overnight. These three individuals reveal just how challenging it can be:

> "The last thing I want to do right now is to love him in any way, shape or form. I would much rather see him reel in pain for what he has said and done to me. To be perfectly honest, I wouldn't care if he dropped off the face of the earth."

> "Turn the other cheek? Are you kidding me?! I would rather slap her in the face! I wanna make her feel the hurt she has caused my family and me. I want her to admit what she has done, apologize and mean it."

"I hate his righteous anger and always coming at me as a know-it-all expert, especially when talking politics. His tone of moral superiority makes me sick. I just wanna shake him until he finally wakes up and sees the truth about how he is acting and what is really going on."

As it was in biblical times and today, these three persons are given full backing to:

- ~ Hate their enemies and retaliate with an eye for an eye and a tooth for a tooth mentality.

- ~ Fight against them with angry words and deeds.

- ~ Harbor resentment in their hearts indefinitely while wishing some form of punishment upon them in return for what they have said and done.

The fact is that loving our enemies is not easy and does not happen overnight. It takes a commitment to do whatever we can to build bridges instead of walls—to foster love instead of hate. It means choosing not to drink the poison of anger and resentment over and over again which not only gnaws at our souls, but also closes the door to any future healing that could take place in the relationship.

This chapter invites you to clarify who your enemies are and to discover what you can do to love and forgive them for real.

Identifying your enemies

As you read over the following list, allow the names of persons to come to mind towards whom you harbor at least a modicum of anger, hatred or resentment. Since death ends a life but not a relationship, be sure to include the names of anyone who has died with whom you still have unresolved or unexpressed feelings.

They may be individuals who:

- ~ Do not listen to you or respect what you have to say.
- ~ Won't speak with you anymore.
- ~ Said or did something to hurt you or someone you care deeply about.
- ~ Righteously identify with (as equal to who they are) certain political, social or moral views that are different from yours.
- ~ Have a prideful, self-righteous and know-it-all attitude.
- ~ Judge and criticize you and infer that you are stupid and wrong for thinking, believing and acting as you do.
- ~ Betrayed, rejected or abandoned you.
- ~ Used or abused you either physically, sexually and/or emotionally.
- ~ Fail to accept and appreciate you for who you are.

- Stubbornly refuse to see the truth about themselves, the situation or the topic at hand.
- Won't share their honest feelings nor allow you to share yours.
- Have a personality type that grates on you.
- Are in competition with you.
- Stabbed you in the back when you were not there to defend yourself.
- Other:

How To Go About Loving Your Enemies

Exercise:
Having identified these people by name, choose one person for starters and then select any of the following options that help you begin the process of forgiving and loving him or her for real.

1. Ask God to help you to even consider forgiving your enemies.

Jesus told us to love everybody. He did not say that everyone would love us in return. If the last thing you want to do right now is to let this person off the hook, take your pain and bitterness to God and ask him to soften your heart and give you the desire and capacity to understand and eventually forgive the other. You may need to make this plea several times.

Ask him to help you see the splinter in your own eye

first before noticing the log in your brother's eye. What I have noticed over the years is that the splinter we can't stand in our brother's eye is often the very log that we cannot stand about ourselves. I suspect that we wouldn't be able to recognize it in another if it wasn't also true about ourselves. For example, we may genuinely hate another's self-righteous and know-it-all attitude and feel repulsed by their belief that they possess the total truth about the topic at hand.

Upon inspection, we may come to find out that we too are self-righteous at times and not open to learning from anyone who holds a contrary point of view. Rather than seeking to understand these persons and how they came to believe as they do, we stand apart as absolute judge and jury. As it turns out, if we are open to learning from them, they can actually be gifts shedding light on dark spots within ourselves that need changing.

2. Forgive, but not too quickly. Release your feelings first.

Before you can say for real that you forgive someone, it is very important to let all negative feelings towards this person out of your body. As termites can gradually destroy the foundation of a house, unforgiveness, hate and resentment can slowly eat away at your soul and body. In the words of Nelson Mandela, the former African revolutionary and anti-apartheid political leader,

> "Resentment is like drinking poison and then hoping it will kill your enemies."[1]

Exercise:
Allow yourself to feel and release any feelings of anger, hate and resentment by doing such things as writing

out your feelings in a journal, expressing your feelings aloud to God, pounding a pillow, talking your feelings out with a friend or confidante or perhaps speaking with the individual directly towards whom you have these feelings.

Whatever way(s) you choose, remember that when you allow yourself to feel with the intention of letting the feelings go, you heal. A sign that you have truly forgiven someone is whenever you think of this person or come into his or her presence, and no longer have these strong negative feelings.

3. Pray, bless and do good to those who hate, curse or mistreat you.

Jesus said, "But to you who are listening I say: Love your enemies, do good to those who hate you, bless those who curse you, pray for those who mistreat you." (Luke 6:27-28). Since we cannot change their minds and hearts, we pray for and bless them trusting that God alone knows what will reach them, open their minds and soften their hearts.

4. Engage the practice of love with them.

Find common ground and interests that you still have together and meet them there. Whether from a distance or in person, love them as they are bringing an expanded space of openness and warmth for them to speak freely and be themselves without fear of being judged or given unsolicited advice.

> Remember that others do best and are most likely to hear a speck of truth when they feel accepted, listened to and blessed by you.

Your acceptance of them does not mean that you agree with them, condone all their ideas or actions, like them or need to be around them. Nor does it mean that you remain silent without expressing your honest thoughts and feelings. Rather, it means that you can agree to disagree while doing your best to listen to them with open eyes, an open mind and a softened heart and to respond in a respectful and caring way. It means that you are open to learn something from them.

If you choose to speak with the individual in person, on the phone or on a face-to-face internet platform, it means engaging such good communication skills as:

- ~ Waiting until the individual is completely finished speaking before responding.
- ~ Asking questions to draw out more information and feeling.
- ~ Repeating back what you heard the other say in your own words so that he or she will know that you have heard them correctly.

Once you take the time to hear their story and learn more about what makes them tick, you will better understand how they came to believe what they believe, even if what they believe is incorrect or missing important pieces of the puzzle. You will also gain insight into why they did or said what they did and be better able to empathize with and eventually forgive them.

5. Walk a mile in their shoes.

> "Judge no man until you've walked a mile in his moccasins."
>
> ~ Indian proverb

Try this exercise to help you walk a mile in another's shoes:

- ~ Choose one person from your list with whom to have a written dialogue.

- ~ Write down as many major chapters from his or her life that you know.

- ~ After listing their major chapters, read them over fairly quickly until you feel the thread of continuity or life-flow that connects all of these major events together; until you get a sense of how these chapters have led them to do and say the things that have hurt you or someone close to you.

- ~ Put your initials down on the left hand side of the paper and begin speaking with the other by writing down whatever is on your mind and heart.

- ~ Next, record the other's initials and record whatever he or she says in reply. Continue speaking back and forth until the conversation naturally comes to a close.

Once the dialogue is complete, write down any feelings or insights that come to you. Empathize with them as best you can knowing that, like you, they are where they are today because of their unique life experiences and relationships.

6. See them through God's eyes.

> "For the Lord sees not as man sees; for man looks on the outward appearance, but the Lord looks on the heart."
>
> ~ 1 Samuel 16:7

Instead of focusing on their faults and wrongdoings and writing them off, feel each of their hearts which may be hurting and longing for someone to accept, care and listen to them. If they are miserable inside, know that their misery will likely spill over onto you and others as well. Remember that God loves each of them and needs you to be there in love for these people in need.

Through God's eyes:

- ~ Focus on who they really are (i.e., children of God), the good they have done in the past, the good they are doing now and the positive potential that lies ahead for them. Know that God is rooting for them and wants you to root for them too.

- ~ Forgive them as fully as you can for what they have done or failed to do realizing that they could not have acted differently because either they did not know any better at the time or lacked the information, insight or wisdom needed to choose differently.

Summary

Growing in greater love of difficult people in your life does not happen overnight. Rather, it means doing whatever you can and for as long as it takes, to love them in spite of whatever they may have said or done that makes you want to harbor resentment and sprint in the opposite direction.

Growing in greater love of these persons takes courage and is fostered by doing such healing things as:

- ~ Asking God to help you want to forgive them when all you feel like doing is punishing them and wishing them ill.

- ~ Allowing yourself to feel and release any feelings of anger, hate and resentment you have towards them, knowing that when you feel, you heal.

- ~ Stopping all effort to change them via rational arguments and emotional pleadings knowing that only God knows what can change their hearts and minds.

- ~ Peacefully agreeing to disagree on certain topics while doing your best to listen to them fully and respond in a respectful and caring way.

- ~ Empathizing with them as fully as you can by walking a mile in their shoes and even taking on some of their sufferings and pain to help lighten their load.

- ~ Realizing that they are likely feeling miserable inside and it is spilling over onto you and others.

- Finding common ground and interests that you still have with them and meeting them there.

- Engaging the practice of love by accepting and blessing them as they are and by bringing an expanded space of openness and warmth for them to speak freely and be themselves without fear of being judged or given unsolicited advice.

- Praying for and blessing them trusting that God alone knows what will reach them and soften their hearts.

- Staying connected with them in the heart versus emotionally dissociating from them in a mood of anger or betrayal.

By doing whatever you can to move from bitterness to forgiveness and from hatred and resentment to love, you are keeping the soil fertile for the possibility of these relationships being healed and growing more deeply over time.

TEN

The Art of Growing in Greater Love of Others

The principle way of growing in love of others is to take on the practice of love.

If you've come this far in the book, it will come as no surprise that the principle way of growing in love of others is to consistently engage the practice of love. It is about building trust by welcoming and accepting others as they are, being fully and calmly present and providing a compassionate and expanded space of love for them to speak freely and be themselves without fear of being judged.

Secondly, it is about listening empathetically to what they are really saying, needing, wanting and feeling with open eyes, an open mind and a softened heart. Once these have been made known, the third step is responding to what you hear with a "How can I serve you?" attitude.

A lack of engaged listening has reached epidemic proportions.

Have you noticed that very few individuals in the public and private arenas have learned the skill of engaged listening? In the public arena, for example, we observe a host of politicians more interested in pushing their personal and party's agendas and in getting elected and gaining power and money, than in actively listening to their constituents and each other with the sincere intention of seeking authentic truth, doing what is right and promoting the common good.

In the private arena, whether at home, school, work or in our church and social groups, we frequently encounter persons doing more talking and preaching than taking the time to really listen to one another and engage in open and honest dialogue. The message is crystal clear: if you want to love better and enhance the quality of all your key relationships, you need to do all you can to master the art of engaged listening.

Why is it that people pay therapists billions of dollars each year just to listen to them? Because they are dying to be listened to and to be in relationship with someone who cares and they can trust. They simply want someone to empathize with them, be genuine and vulnerable themselves and give them the positive energy and acceptance they crave.

Despite the fact that people spend more time listening than they do in any form of communication, the average untrained listener actually hears only 25% of what is being said. The rest of the time is spent daydreaming or thinking about what his or her next response will be.

Those who learn how to listen well with genuine empathy stand the best chance of having good personal and business relationships. To illustrate this point, I asked my brother, a very successful retired printing salesman, what the secret was to his success:

"I listened. That was basically it," he said. "I listened closely to what my clients wanted and needed and then did my best to give them exactly that. If they had unaired fears about such things as the cost of the job or if it would be completed according to specs and on time, I simply invited them to express their fears and just listened. Once they let out their feelings, I addressed their concerns as honestly as I could. As a result, they typically became more relaxed, more trusting and more open to listening to what I had to offer and to move forward in the process."

No one is born with the ability to listen skillfully—it must be learned.

Whereas hearing is a natural process that is done unconsciously and automatically, listening must be learned. It is a selective process made up of those sounds and bodily gestures we choose to pay attention to. Mary Kay Ash, the founder of the Mary Kay line of cosmetics and one of the greatest women entrepreneurs of all time, affirms the necessity of teaching this very important skill:

> "All through school, we're taught to read, write, and speak; yet we're never taught to listen . . . the most undervalued of all the communication skills." [1]

Relationships struggle when:

> Husbands and wives
> Parents and children
> Siblings
> In-laws
> Teachers and students
> Bosses and employees
> Salespeople and clients
> Clergy and parishioners
> Health care workers and patients
> Radio/TV hosts and their guests
> Politicians
> Leaders and their constituents

do *not* actively listen to each other.

When active listening is *not* present, it's akin to:

- ~ Two people talking at each other without caring what the other has to say.
- ~ Arriving to a discussion dressed in full suits of armor, ready to ward off the other in battle.
- ~ Me showing up, ready to give you my point of view in hopes that you will change yours because mine has solid reasoning, facts and even God behind it.

The bottom line is that the failure to actively listen hinders the quality of communication and thus weakens relationships. Conversely, when active listening is present with both individuals genuinely seeking to arrive at the truth and working towards a solution, relationships are strengthened.

Love better by becoming the best listener and communicator you can be.

> Listening and communicating well is love in action.

The focus of this chapter is to help you become the best listener and communicator you can be so that you can love better and have happier and healthier relationships.

Although the assessments and tips offered here for better listening and communicating provide the self-awareness and information needed to greatly improve your listening and communication skills, the chapter is by no means a complete presentation of the subject.

At our **Love in Action:** *Becoming the Best Listener and Communicator You Can Be* workshops, for example, we go into greater depth about the subject and offer participants hands-on exercises to further deepen their listening and communication skills—to enhance their ability to love.

As you go through the following five steps to becoming a skilled listener and communicator, be on the lookout for ways you can increase your skills. To the extent that you learn and habitually practice any of these skills, the quality of your life and relationships will be greatly enhanced.

While so doing, be patient with yourself, understanding that it takes time and practice to become good at anything, which includes becoming skilled at listening and communicating.

Love in Action ~ Five Steps to Becoming the Best Listener and Communicator You Can Be:

Step 1: Become aware of your listening blocks.

Most people believe that if they hear with their ears and speak with their mouths, that they are good listeners and communicators. However, the truth is that we all have blocks that prevent us from listening and communicating well. Let us begin with our listening blocks.

These blocks have already damaged some of our relationships and will continue to do so in the future until we become aware of what these blocks are and begin doing the opposite and forming good listening habits. To identify your blocks to listening, take the following *Listening Blocks Assessment*.

Listening Blocks Assessment

Scoring: 1 = Never   2 = Rarely   3 = Sometimes
          4 = Often   5 = Always

1. ___ Think about what I am going to say next while the other is speaking, hardly waiting before jumping in with my viewpoint or rebuttal.

2. ___ Decide ahead of time that my ideas are correct and that what the other has to say is irrelevant or incorrect.

3. ___ Allow negative judgments and feelings I already have about the person and their opinions to overshadow what is being said.

The Art of Growing in Greater Love of Others

4. ___ Judge ahead of time that the speaker is incompetent and does not know what he or she is talking about.

5. ___ Focus on such things as the speaker's personality, looks, voice and delivery, and thus block out what the other is saying.

6. ___ Determine ahead of time that the subject is boring, irrelevant or too difficult for me to understand.

7. ___ Daydream while pretending that I am really interested in what the other has to say.

8. ___ Talk too much and dominate the conversation.

9. ___ Allow emotionally charged words to affect me so that I block out the content of what the other is saying.

10. ___ Listen for what I want to hear and what will support my preconceptions, instead of what is actually being said.

11. ___ Be so busy and preoccupied with what I'm doing at the moment that I don't take time to stop and really listen.

12. ___ Let distractions (i.e., my cell phone, someone else walking into the room) and other interruptions get in the way of truly listening to the other.

Now that you've identified your listening blocks, begin observing when these blocks come up while conversing with others and simply do the opposite. Once you do, you will notice that your conversations will be more relaxed, interesting and engaging. To become an even better listener, begin practicing the following tips.

Step 2: Practice these tips to become a better listener:

1. **Be fully present.**

    Be 100% focused. Simply listen; refrain from doing anything else.

    Look at the person. People tend not to trust anyone who won't look at them.

    Face the speaker square on. This posture shows you want to understand.

    Lean forward. Shows interest in what the other is saying.

    Nod your head occasionally and make responses such as:

    "Uh-huh ..."   *"I see ..."*   *"Hmm ..."*

    Let your face speak. Facial expressions show you are reacting to what is said.

    Also,

    ~ **Disregard distractions** by doing such things as muting your cell phone, taking off your ear buds and ignoring noises and people walking by.

- **Refrain from daydreaming** when the subject matter seems either boring, irrelevant or too difficult to understand or when you may not like the speaker's voice, looks, personality or delivery. Instead, listen for what the speaker is really saying, feeling and needing.

- **Don't change the subject** because once you do, the person who was cut off may not offer any more ideas and will likely find a reason to leave your presence.

- **Listen with your body,** even on the telephone. Sit erect as poor body positions are not conducive to effective listening.

2. **Listen to understand vs. listen to reply.**

Before speaking with another about a topic of importance, do your best to empty yourself of any lingering feelings and ideas and even quiet your inspirations in order to be as present as possible.

Rather than trying to make your point or win the argument, be silent and listen calmly with an open mind and heart allowing the speaker to get out his or her entire message without interrupting.

Trusting that the other is longing to be heard and understood, resist the urge to jump into the middle of a conversation when you get an idea, want to correct the other or are reminded of something by the other's words.

Also, do your best to walk a mile in the other's shoes by empathetically feeling and seeing things from their point of view before sharing your own. By practicing full-on empathy in this way:

- You are literally taking in what the other is feeling to the point where their burdens can be somewhat relieved or their joys expanded.

- You will not only understand the person better, but also give the other an experience of empathetic understanding which may inspire him or her to respond in a similar way.

3. **Say only what needs to be said** because most of the time the main cause of arguments is over something that was said. Instead of yielding to the temptation to say whatever pops into your head, learn to speak less and say only what is necessary. By so doing, you will have more peace and less misunderstanding.

4. **Ask questions** to help the person figure out their situation better or to pull out more emotion and how they think. Rather than giving answers, asking questions helps elicit further reflection and new understanding in the listener.

Have you noticed that answers tend to close and questions open? Compared to closed questions which elicit one-word answers such as "yes" or "no", open-ended questions require the person being asked to expand

The Art of Growing in Greater Love of Others

on the topic. Some examples of open-ended questions are:

"What do you think about . . .?"
"Why do you think . . .?"
"How would you do that differently?"
"What is your biggest challenge with . . .?"
"What other specific details can you give me?"

Since our stories connect us, try asking the question, "What's your story?", and then sit back and listen until the story comes to a natural end. Likewise, when someone tells you something that is not in your belief system, resist the urge to stop the p e r s o n midstream to correct them or show them how they are wrong. Instead, ask "How did you arrive at this belief?" and then listen attentively.

If you really want to get to know someone, ask them good questions during the flow of any conversation and then stop and listen seeking to understand and learn something that you may not have known before. Why? Because most people want to know how much you care before they want to know how much you know.

Asking questions shows that you genuinely care and goes a long way in strengthening your relationship.

Have you noticed that people only truly believe what they say and not what you say? Therefore, if you want to help others see a particular truth, ask questions, listen and ask more questions until the truth rolls off of their lips rather than your own.

Jesus and Socrates mastered the art of asking questions.

Rather than answering questions directly, which he did only three times in the Gospels, Jesus chose instead to ask 307 different questions and to speak in parables in order to transform and elicit new understanding in his listeners. [2]

5. **Summarize in *your own words*** what the other is saying so that the person can tell you if you heard them correctly. Rather than repeating back their exact words like a parrot, simply speak back what you heard them say by using such expressions as:

    "What I hear you saying is . . ."
    "So what we've agreed to is . . ."
    "Are you saying that . . . ?"
    "Let me see if I'm hearing you correctly . . ."

    Similarly, to draw out how the other is feeling about a particular issue, use such empathy responses as:

    "You sound upset."
    "You seem ... (feeling word)."
    "You look ... (feeling word)."

Summarizing is arguably the most important listening tip because when others know for sure that they are being heard correctly, they not only feel cared for (i.e., loved), but are also more apt to return the favor by making sure they are hearing you correctly as well.

Such repeating back or summarizing need only take place in more serious conversations so that what is being said can be understood and appropriate action can be taken if necessary.

Since listening with the ear of the heart is step two of the practice of love, putting these listening skills into practice will go a long way in helping you love and relate better with others. To increase your listening skills even further, read the following to learn how to listen with your eyes and recognize the non-verbal messages coming from the body language of others.

Step 3: Pay attention to non-verbal messages.

The body never lies. Words, on the other hand...

It is important to look for clues as to what the other is actually communicating and feeling but not saying in words. Such clues are found by listening with your eyes to the body language (i.e., the nonverbal messages) rather than listening solely to the words.

It is estimated that the majority of communication is non-verbal with posture, facial expression, pitch and volume being far more reliable indicators of what a person is actually feeling and thinking than the words themselves.

Once you notice the body expressing non-verbal messages and feelings, here are some phrases to help you increase clarity and build rapport between you and the speaker. For example,

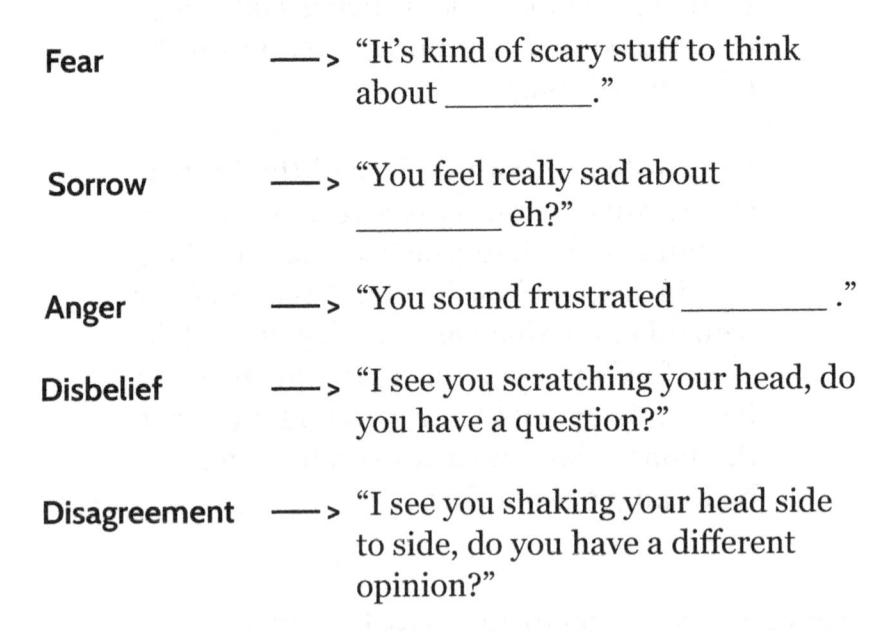

Fear	—>	"It's kind of scary stuff to think about _____."
Sorrow	—>	"You feel really sad about _____ eh?"
Anger	—>	"You sound frustrated _____."
Disbelief	—>	"I see you scratching your head, do you have a question?"
Disagreement	—>	"I see you shaking your head side to side, do you have a different opinion?"

These feeding back phrases invite the speaker to go more into depth about whatever he or she may be feeling. Here are some nonverbal messages that our bodies convey and the interpretations revealing what they are typically, but not always, feeling behind the message.

Although the nonverbal messages and interpretations presented here will help you become a more accurate listener, this section is offered solely as an introduction to the subject. If you'd like to delve more deeply into this key facet of communication, further research on body language is encouraged.

Nonverbal Message	Feeling
Making direct eye contact	Friendly, sincere, extroverted, secure, self-confident, assertive, telling the truth
Avoiding eye contact	Cold, evasive, indifferent, insecure, passive, lying frightened, or nervous
Nodding head up and down	Agreement or understanding
Shaking head side to side	Disagreement, shock or disbelief
Flaring nostrils	Anger or frustration
Leaning forward	Attentive or interested
Scratching the head	Bewilderment or disbelief
Smiling	Agreement or contentment
Narrowing eyes	Disagreement, resentment, anger or disapproval
Slouching in the seat	Bored or relaxed

Nonverbal Message	**Feeling**
Yawning	Bored
Folded arms or placing hands on hips	Resistant, disapproval, defensiveness, anger
A shrug of the shoulders	Unsure
Biting the lip	Fearful, nervous, anxious
Wringing hands	Fearful, nervous, anxious
Crunched up nose, raised up chin, clenched fist,	Angry
Holding of breath	Hiding something
Touching nose	Hiding something
Voice drops in tone	Lack of confidence in what is being said
Fingers over the lip	Fear of telling the truth
Throat swallowing	Fear
Eyebrows pulled together	Fear
Looking down and away	Shame or guilt

Congratulations! You have already become a better listener by becoming aware of your listening blocks, learning excellent tips for how to listen better and by increasing your ability to pick up on what others are really saying and feeling by listening to their body language.

Remember, every time you do your best to empathetically listen to others and then act on what you hear with a serving attitude, you are actively engaging the practice of love and enhancing your relationship. How important is good communication? If you do not listen and communicate well, you will not love well. In contrast, listening and communicating well is love in action. To continue growing in your ability to become a skilled communicator, read on.

Step 4: Switch from sending "You" Messages to "I" Messages.

Too often, when we must tell someone about his or her performance or behavior, especially if it is unacceptable, we use "You" messages which sound something like this:

> "Jack, you missed your objectives again. You need to see what you can do differently to improve your performance."

> or

> "Sarah, you have gotten low grades on three tests in a row. You need to get some help before the next test, OK?"

"You" messages point the finger and can be received as blame, criticism and even rejection. They can also cause the other to feel angry and become reactively resistant to changing their behavior. In short, "You" messages should be avoided because they seldom do what they are intended to accomplish—to influence a person to change

The Practice of Love

his or her unacceptable behavior.

To identify the particular "You" messages that you tend to use at times when addressing someone's unacceptable behavior, take the following "You" Messages Assessment.

"You" Messages Assessment

Scoring: 1 = Never   2 = Rarely   3 = Sometimes
          4 = Often   5 = Always

When addressing someone's unacceptable behavior, I tend to:

1. __ **Judge, criticize, disagree, blame.** ("You acted foolishly ..." "You're not thinking straight ..." " What were you thinking?!")

2. __ **Advise, suggest, solve.** ("What I would do is ..." "Why don't you ...")

3. __ **Moralize, preach, oblige.** ("You should ..." "You ought to ..." "It's your responsibility ...")

4. __ **Order, direct, command.** ("You must ..." "You have to ...")

5. __ **Persuade with logic, argue, teach, lecture.** ("Yes, but ..." "Do you realize ..." "Here's why you're wrong ...")

6. __ **Interpret, analyze, diagnose.** ("What you need is ..." "Your problem is ..." "You mean ...")

7. __ **Warn, promise, threaten.** ("You had better ..." "If you don't, then ...")

8. ___	Name-call, ridicule, shame.	("You're a sloppy worker ..." "You've screwed up ..." "You always ..." or "You never ...")
9. ___	Probe, question, interrogate.	("Why ...?" "Who ...?" "What ...?")
10. ___	Withdraw, distract, divert, use humor.	("Let's discuss it later ..." "That reminds me of the time ..." "I don't want to talk about it!")
11. ___	Reassure, sympathize, console, support.	("Don't worry ..." "You'll feel better ..." "It's not so bad ...")
12. ___	Praise, agree, evaluate positively, approve by me-tooing.	("Don't listen to them, you've done a good job ..." "You're right, they're wrong ..." "The same thing happened to me ...")

Now that you've become aware of what "You" messages you have tended to use in the past, you are now free to stop communicating in this way and to use "I" statements instead.

What are "I" statements and how can they be used to elicit a positive change in behavior?

"I" statements can be used to make people aware of their unacceptable behavior in a non-blaming and non-judgmental way. They are a way of taking ownership of your feelings when giving feedback to someone.

Each "I" statement contains the following four components:

1. A brief description of the behavior you find good or unacceptable.

2. Your honest feelings about the behavior stating the degree of emotional impact that the behavior had on you.

3. The tangible concrete effect of the behavior on you or your organization.

4. Asking the person what they think needs to be done or what needs to happen so that the unacceptable behavior can change in the future.

Using these four components tells the person that you really have a logical reason for wanting the behavior to change.

An easy formula to remember is as follows:

1. **When you . . .** (description of performance/behavior)

2. **I feel . . .** (your feeling(s))

3. **because . . .** (the specific effects)

4. **"What do you think needs to happen for you to . . . ?"**

    (when dealing with unacceptable behavior)

Examples about what to say when you want the behavior *to change*:

1. When you — come to work 30 minutes late,

2. I feel — frustrated,

3. because — I have to cover for you and can't get my own work done.

4. Going forward, what do you think needs to happen — for you to consistently get to work on time?

1. When you — fail to meet your production goals three months in a row,

2. I feel — very concerned,

3. because — it lowers the overall productivity of the entire office.

4. What do you think needs to happen — for you to consistently meet your production goals in the near future?

Examples about what to say when you want the behavior *to continue*:

1. When you	write down all your assignments and complete them on time,
2. I feel	encouraged,
3. because	I know you're on top of it. Keep up the good work!
1. When you	help out around the house and walk the dogs,
2. I feel	grateful
3. because	it helps all of us. Thanks for helping out.

At first, sending "I" statements may seem mechanical or make you feel self-conscious. With practice, however, "I" messages will come more naturally and require less deliberate thought. To learn more about how to improve your communication skills, consider the recommendations offered in Step 5.

Step 5: Practice these tips to become a better communicator:

1. Be positive in your speech and tone of voice and thus avoid:

- ~ Joining in other people's suffering by sharing wounds and similar problems from your own life.

- ~ Retelling painful events and past traumas.

- ~ Greeting others with whatever mood you happen to be in at the time.

- ~ Saying something negative when people ask you how you are (i.e., talk about your tiredness, problems, aches or pains).

- ~ Talking about negative events that are happening.

- ~ Being negative (i.e., pessimistic, critical, argumentative, sarcastic or cynical) in your speech and tone of voice.

- ~ Gossiping or spreading rumors about others when they are not present to defend themselves. Have you noticed that people tend to lower their voice when they start talking negatively about others?

- ~ Joining in when absent people are being put down.

Once again, since we become what we focus on, it is important to stay positive and upbeat with your words and tone of voice. By so doing, you will not only feel better, but others will feel better too and be happy to be around you. Thus, avoid negative people and surround yourself instead with positive individuals of high integrity who naturally encourage you to be the real you.

2. Create rapport with people by:

- ~ Matching their tone and energy level.
- ~ Finding ways of connecting with them as they are in that moment.
- ~ Talking about what interests them rather than what might be of interest to you.

3. Ask for what you need.

- ~ **Be direct.** "Please be at the meeting at 9 a.m. sharp."
- ~ **Be specific.** "I need your report in by closing time on Thursday."
- ~ **Be firm.** Don't apologize for asking. Just ask.
- ~ **Be respectful.** Ask, don't tell and use "please" and "thank you."

4. Say what you mean and want and thus avoid:

- ~ Being afraid to say what you mean and want and dancing around the truth.
- ~ Being wishy-washy and playing both sides of a situation by saying things you don't really think and feel just to keep the peace or gain approval.

- Saying "yes" when you mean "no" out of fear of offending others.

- Exaggerating, bragging or changing facts about your life story to impress others or gain some advantage.

Since others cannot read your mind, when you clearly say what you mean and want, those listening to you can relax because your desire is clear. For example, when you say "I would love pancakes for breakfast", I can happily set about making them for you knowing that pancakes is exactly what you want.

5. Be slow to share personal information about yourself, your family or what you value and believe in most deeply until others show they can be trusted and won't use what you shared against you in some way. **Trust needs to be earned.**

6. If you want to have the best chance of someone listening to you and accepting your message, pick the right time and place away from distractions and outside the heat of battle and then speak the truth only with love.

> "Truth is vital, but truth without love is unbearable."
>
> ~ Unknown author

Have you noticed that:

- Spewing the facts or the law at others (especially with righteous anger or coming across as a know-it-all expert with a tone of moral superiority) does not inspire them to change?

- ~ Judging others either verbally or in your mind actually pushes them away from ever hearing whatever modicum of truth you might have to convey?

On the other hand, have you noticed that:

- ~ You are most open to hearing the truth from someone you have a relationship with and can trust?

- ~ You are most apt to listen to and take to heart what someone says when you feel accepted by the other and when the other is genuine, vulnerable and free of righteous judgment?

- ~ Speaking the truth without love is actually harmful while sharing the truth in love offers a better chance of that truth being heard, accepted and acted upon?

7. When someone asks for your advice, refrain from saying what you think the other should do. Instead, ask the person, "What do *you* think you should do?" They most often come up with the solution that feels right to them and leave feeling satisfied and appreciative for you giving them the opportunity to access their own truth.

When someone asks your opinion about what you think they should do relative to their life's work, here's what a wise 92-year-old man had to say: "Your calling is 100% between you and God. If I veer you off from that consideration and conversation by even 2% by stating what *I* think you should do, that is 2% too much."

8. When someone is spewing anger at you, try turning their vitriol back into a restatement of what they said. By so doing, you can defuse the anger and turn it into an honest debate and discussion. Always remember that there's a person behind all those negative words and reactivity in need of being heard and understood.

9. Are you in a relationship with someone who feels deeply hurt by what you've done or not done in the past? Has the person been wounded so badly that it seems like there is but a small chance for the wound to be healed? As a result, are you both walking around feeling unloved, unappreciated and uncared for? If yes, using the example of a wife being deeply hurt by her husband, consider doing something like this:

~ Allow your wife to express her feelings of anger, resentment and bitterness without chiming in, defending or analyzing what is being said. Do your best to feel her pain.

~ To let her know that you have heard how she feels, repeat back what you heard her say in your own words. If she says that you still do not fully grasp how she is feeling or what she has been through, invite her to tell you again what you might've missed and then listen carefully without interrupting.

Once your conversation comes to an end and you have departed company, if you feel that she still does not feel totally heard, write down all that you heard her say. When the time is right, read it back to her empathetically and give her the opportunity to tell you if you heard her correctly.

~ In the days and months ahead, resist the urge to focus on how you are not getting your needs met like you would like or how unloved, unappreciated or uncared for you feel. Instead, put the other first by consistently **loving over the top for as long as it takes** knowing that if you want to change a big hurt, you have to make a big change. Most of all, be patient. It may take several weeks or months for true healing to occur. Although it may take longer than you would like, is it not worth the wait?

10. When saying good-bye to someone, remember that the last impression and feeling is what people will remember. Therefore, leave them feeling heard and appreciated.

> "At the end of the day people won't remember what you said or did, they will remember how you made them feel."
> ~ Maya Angelou

Also, whenever possible, talk things through instead of going to bed angry. However, if you do go to bed angry, hit the reset button when you awaken. You might do that by giving the other a hug or, if needed, allowing unexpressed feelings and issues from the night before to be fully aired out.

11. Before you speak, act or make that phone call, ask yourself: Is what I am about to say or do going to build the relationship up or tear it down? Is it going to make the other feel good, guilty or bad? Then, speak or act *only* if it will build the relationship up.

12. Avoid saying things that can result in misunderstandings and conflict when communicating via text messaging, mail or email.

Since most of what we say is heard through non-verbal means of communication (body language, tone, pitch, emotion), it is better, whenever possible, to convey emotional messages in person. Why? Because the other will inevitably misinterpret your words, read between the lines and completely miss subtle shades of meaning and intention that can only be gotten through in-person verbal and non-verbal communication.

Thus, the basic rule is to use face-to-face communication when expressing emotional content so that the full array of verbal and non-verbal expressions can be experienced by both parties and the message can be clearly delivered and received with less chance of being misunderstood.

13. Show and tell your family often how much you love and appreciate them. Try greeting every family member who walks through the door with a warm welcome that would make your dog proud.

Upon Reflection:

~ Do you believe that the quality of your communication has a great impact on the quality of your life and relationships?

~ From the self-awareness and information you've acquired in this chapter, do you feel equipped to begin applying what you've learned in your relationships so that you can grow in your ability to listen and communicate more effectively?

~ Do you truly want to become the best listener and communicator you can be and thus love better?

If you answered "yes" to these questions, all that's left is for you is to begin putting into practice what you've learned, one or two actions at a time. Since practicing good listening and speaking skills is love in action, every small action you take will not only improve the quality of your communication but also the quality of your life and relationships as well.

ELEVEN

A Side-By-Side Comparison of When You Are and Are Not Engaging the Practice of Love with Others

You *are* engaging the Practice of Love with others when you are:

~ Welcoming and accepting of them as they are.

~ Fully and calmly present providing an expanded space of openness and warmth for them to speak freely and be themselves.

~ Caring and taking the time to listen and understand without judging and giving unsolicited advice.

You *are not* engaging the Practice of Love with others when you are:

~ Unwelcoming, unaccepting and critical of them or write them off.

~ Distracted and reactive with a closed mind and heart not allowing them to speak freely and be themselves.

~ Listening to reply and give advice without taking the time to really listen and understand.

~ Listening to their fears, frustrations, wants and needs and ready to respond to what you hear with a "How can I serve you?" attitude.

~ Focused primarily on getting your own wants and needs met with a "What's in it for me?" attitude.

~ Focused on whether or not you are feeling loved, cared for, wanted, paid attention to, needed or desirable and then feeling betrayed and reacting negatively when you are not.

You *are* engaging the Practice of Love with others when you are:

You *are not* engaging the Practice of Love with others when you are:

~ Empathetically attuned to the truth of whatever is being communicated both verbally and non-verbally in your conversations and dealings with others.

~ Resistant to hearing the truth of whatever is being communicated in your conversations and dealings with others

~ Making your relationships stronger by thinking, saying and doing things that build relationships up.

~ Making your relationships weaker by thinking, saying and doing things that tear relationships down.

A Side-By-Side Comparison

"Therefore, encourage one another and build one another up." ~1 Thes. 5:11

~ Practicing good listening and communication skills.
~ Not practicing good listening and communication skills.

~ Forgiving, but not too quickly, allowing yourself to feel through your feelings first.
~ Holding on to your resentment by feeling the same negative feelings over and over again.

~ Unselfish and share what you have.
~ Selfish and portion things out.

~ Cooperative.
~ Uncooperative.

~ Open, honest, transparent.
~ Closed, dishonest, secretive.

~ Patient.
~ Impatient.

~ Not easily angered.
~ Easily angered.

~ Trusting.
~ Untrusting, worrying.

~ Kind — sensitive to their feelings.
~ Unkind — insensitive to their feelings.

~ Not jealous.
~ Jealous.

~ Not seeking your own advantage.
~ Seeking your own advantage.

~ Humble.
~ Boastful and proud.

~ Not rude.
~ Rude.

~ Not rejoicing at the wrongdoing or misfortune of others.

~ Rejoicing at the wrongdoing or misfortune of others.

When you *are not* engaging the practice of love notice that . . .

~ Your attention and energy move *inwards* in a self-referencing way.

~ You are primarily focused on your own interests, needs, problems or wants.

~ You are closed to hearing the truth about yourself, the other, the topic at hand or your relationship and acting on what you hear.

~ Your relationships suffer. On the other hand,

When you *are* engaging the practice of love notice that . . .

~ Your attention and energy move outwards in service of others.

~ You are primarily focused on the interests, needs, problems and wants of others and consistently attending to them as best you can with a serving heart.

~ You are open to hearing the truth about yourself, the other, the topic at hand or your relationship and acting on what you hear.

~ Your relationships are strengthened.

"Do nothing out of selfish ambition or vain conceit. Rather, in humility value others above yourselves, not looking out for your own interests, but each of you to the interests of others."

~ Phil. 2:3-4

TWELVE

Moving Forward ~ Cultivating the Art of Growing in Greater Love of Yourself, Others and God

The key to growing in greater love

Years ago, a five-year research study was done to discover the key ingredients to becoming a successful baseball player. Great players from the past and present were interviewed during the process along with the reading of many articles and books and the viewing of videos on the greatest players of all time. What was it that made these players great and others mediocre? Coaches and players from all the competitive sports and other venues awaited their findings with high anticipation.

While natural ability, being in excellent physical condition, being coachable and utilizing the best tips offered by sports psychology all played a part, practicing the most came out as the number one ingredient that propelled these athletes to a high level of excellence. On game days, these players would typically arrive early to the park to work on certain aspects of their trade and often stayed after the game as well to hone their skills even more.

The practice of love demands the same level of commitment and practice. Just as great athletes must practice intently to become outstanding at their trade, we also must:

~ Become aware of whatever we need to do in order to love better and then act on that awareness one step at a time with courage, consistency and a servant's heart.

~ Engage the practice of love on a daily basis and hone our relationship skills in order to become the best listener, communicator and lover we can be.

Becoming aware is step one in the growth process. **Step two is taking consistent action.** For example, if you become aware of what you specifically need to do to listen and communicate better, and then follow that up by consistently putting those listening and communication skills into practice, you and your relationships grow.

On the other hand, if you become aware but do not consistently act on that awareness, you do not grow and your old way of relating gets more problematic as time goes on. As the saying goes, "If you do not make any changes, nothing changes."

Awareness + Consistent Action = Growth

Three relationships are strengthened whenever you engage the practice of love.

It is encouraging to know that whenever you engage the practice of love by doing your best to listen to God and then follow his guidance in service of your neighbor, three relationships are strengthened in the process:

One: When you consistently listen to God (i.e., the Spirit of truth) speaking in the depths of your conscience nudging you to think, say or do that which is right, true and good, and then act on what you hear in loving service, you deepen your love of God.

Two: Once you act on what you hear by concretely serving another through supportive words and actions or just being present, you strengthen your relationship with that person.

Three: After listening to God and then responding by serving another, you feel good about yourself and thus grow in genuine self-love.

In diagram form it looks like this:

Listen to God ⟶	**Become** ⟶	**Act** ⟶	**Grow in**
(i.e., the Spirit of truth) in the depths of your conscience	**aware of the truth** about yourself, another, a situation or the topic at hand	**consistently on that truth** in loving service	**greater love** of God, others and yourself

As long as you are doing your best to listen for the truth and act on what you hear in your encounters, work and circumstances of everyday life, you will gradually build up your listening and acting muscles. By seeking to do what is right and true in the small things, you will gradually become more adept at making God-guided choices when the bigger decisions come along like discerning your career path, the person you are to marry or how to invest your money.

Genuine love involves a commitment to love on purpose.

Love is not just a feeling nor measured by how much positive emotion you may be feeling about an other at any given time. While loving feelings are indeed present and appreciated at various times over the course of a relationship, they are fleeting and not the foundation that keeps it alive.

If you tend to think that love is about having someone else make you feel better, you will be disappointed and possibly even leave the relationship when many of your needs are not met, when it is no longer as fun and gratifying or when multiple disagreements take place.

Genuine love, on the other hand, is a choice rather than something you fall into and out of. It involves a commitment to consistently do your best to:

- ~ Lead with love rather than judgment by welcoming and blessing whoever is before you.

- ~ Provide a judgment-free space of acceptance and openness for others to speak freely and be themselves.

- ~ Be fully and calmly present listening for the truth that the other may be conveying with an open mind and a softened heart and then to respond to what you hear with a serving disposition.

~ Make your relationships stronger by putting others first.

~ Ask for forgiveness, including from your children, and forgive yourself whenever your thoughts, words and actions have been less than loving.

- Engaging the practice of love with others is not about loving perfectly and then feeling guilty when you do not. It is not about being the perfect friend, spouse, daughter, son, sibling, in-law, mother or father.

  Rather, it is about doing your best to consistently listen to the needs, wants, fears and frustrations of others and then to respond with caring words, deeds or by simply being present with them.

~ Practice good listening and communication skills so that you become a focused and empathetic listener and a clear and compassionate communicator with all you meet.

It's all about relationship

Now that you have a better sense of what true love is and how to go about growing in greater love of yourself, others and God, you are now in a position to love intentionally; to make positive choices each day to help you love better.

Unlike the self-effort alone paths that put the individual first in an attempt to achieve some personal goals like enlightenment, getting your needs met, or being, doing and having it all, the Jesus path is unique because it's all about relationship.

It's about:

- ~ Seeking first God's wisdom and truth when addressing problems and needs.

- ~ Standing strong in your relationship with God by doing your best to listen to the Spirit of truth speaking through all of creation, sifting out what is true in the depths of your conscience with the guidance of that same Spirit and your spiritual confidante(s) and then responding in loving service over and over again.

- ~ Engaging the practice of love not as a three-step method, but as a lifelong and dynamic relationship with a personal, forgiving and loving God.

- ~ Putting forth self-effort, but the type of self-effort that has God initiating your next steps and then guiding and supporting you each step of the way to love the best you can.

- ~ Making your life less busy, your mind less full and your heart less burdened in order to make space for the living God and his loving guidance in all areas of your life.

- Making a conscious decision each day to bring the practice of love to everyone you meet.

- Dying to yourself by compassionately entering into the sufferings and burdens of others in order to lighten their load.

It's also about:

- Relishing in their joys so that their joys might increase.

- Loving others by doing to them what you would have them do unto you, even if they don't.

- Loving your enemies (i.e., the obstinate neighbor next door, the righteous know-it-all, or the employee or boss who pushes your buttons) as Jesus commanded by consistently engaging the practice of love with them, praying for them often, seeing them the way God sees them, seeking to understand them better by walking a mile in their shoes and forgiving them.

- Seeing everyone as a child of God knowing that they:
  - Are exactly where they are and need to be at the moment.
  - Have unique life experiences that have brought them to where they are right now and thus cannot and should not be anywhere else.

- Do best and are most likely to hear a speck of truth when they feel welcomed, empathetically listened to and loved by you.

~ Building stronger relationships by doing more listening than preaching, more dialoguing than monologuing and more giving than receiving.

~ Teaching others about the practice through word and deed so that the seed of love can be planted and start to grow in the hearts of as many individuals as possible.

~ Knowing in the core of your being that when you come to the end of your life, the quality with which you have loved God, others and yourself will be all that really mattered.

~ Understanding that true relationship is not just about meeting each others' needs and striving to have as pleasurable and stress-free life as possible, but about mutual giving from the heart, putting the other first and helping each other discern God's wishes in matters big and small.

And finally, it is about helping each other know and do all of the above in hopes of obtaining the ultimate treasure of being in ecstatic communion with God and the saints forever in heaven.

Footnotes

Chapter 1   What is the Practice of Love?

[1] Thomas, Andrew, "How Training These Service Dogs Helps Veterans Heal," (The Epoch Times, 9-15 Sept. 2020), pp. 6-7. Used with permission.

Chapter 2   Why Engage the Practice of Love?

[1] 1 Cor. 13:8 Love is eternal, God is love and His love for us is everlasting.

[2] "Albert Schweitzer Quotes," BrainyQuote.com. (BrainyMedia Inc, 2023) 16 July 2023. https://www.brainyquote.com/quotes/albert_schweitzer_387027.

Chapter 3   The Practice of Love and the Jesus Path

[1] Lk. 19:1-10

[2] The story of the Samaritan Woman is found in Jn. 4:4-42

[3] Mt. 22:37-40

[4] Jn. 6:38

[5] Jn. 14:31

[6] Jn. 18:37

[7] Mk. 14:36

[8] Mt. 7:21

[9] Lk. 6:47-48

[10] Mt. 7:24, 26

[11] Lk. 10:38-42

[12] Mt. 6:9-10

Chapter 4   What Stands in the Way of Hearing the Truth?

[1] Jn. 16:7

[2] Jn. 16:12-13

[3] Jn. 8:32

[4] Mk. 10:17-22

[5] Ex. 4:14-16

[6] Acts 7:22

Chapter 5   The Ultimate Choice: Obey God or Chart Your Own Course

[1] **Lewis, C.S**, *The Great Divorce*, (Harper Collins, 2015).

[2] **Russell, Bertrand**, *Power: A New Social Analysis*, 1938, Chapter One, (Unwin Books, 1983).

[3] **Whitman, Walt**, *Songs of Myself*, 48, Leaves of Grass:Unabridged Deathbed Edition with 400 Poems, (Seawolf Press, 2023).

[4] **Carus, Paul** (Editor), *Sayings of Buddha*, (Peter Pauper Press, 1957).

[5] Mt. 4:18-22

Chapter 6   The Art of Growing in Greater Love of God

[1] **Paul VI, Pope,** *Pastoral Constitution on the Church in the Modern World-Gaudium et Spes,* Dec. 7, 1965. Copyright © Libreria Editrice Vaticana. Used with permission.

[2] 1 Thes. 5:21

[3] **Tada, Joni Eareckson,** *Finding God in Hidden Places,* (Harvest House Publishers, 1999), p. 32.

[4] St. Ignatius of Loyola used the words true Spirit and false spirit to differentiate the opposing forces at play when one is engaged in the process of discernment.

[5] For a more detailed explanation of the principles and practice of Ignatian discernment, see **David Lonsdale**'s excellent book entitled *Eyes to See, Ears to Hear—An Introduction to Ignatian Spirituality,* (Orbis Books, 2000), pp. 95ff.

[6] Gal. 5:22-23

[7] **Merton, Thomas,** *Thoughts in Solitude,* (Farrar, Straus and Giroux, 1958), p. 83. Used with permission.

Chapter 7   Five Ways to Help Deepen Your Love of God

[1] **Lubich, Chiara,** *Essential Writings,* (New City Press, 2007), p. 102.

[2] You can read the original description of Imaginative Contemplation in *The Spiritual Exercises of Ignatius of Loyola* composed between 1522–1524 by **St. Ignatius of Loyola**, a 16th-century Spanish priest, theologian and founder of the Society of Jesus (Jesuits).

[3] Ps. 46:10

[4] St. Teresa of Calcutta, *In the Heart of the World: Thoughts, Stories and Prayers*, (New World Library, 1997).

[5] 1 Thes. 5:18

[6] Col. 2:7

[7] "Finding God in all things" is a central theme in the spirituality of St. Ignatius of Loyola.

[8] Brother Lawrence's wonderful book, *The Practice of the Presence of God*, offers simple and practical ways of recalling God's presence in everyday life.

[9] Hutchinson, Gloria, *A Retreat with Gerald Manley Hopkins and Hildegard of Bingen*, (St. Anthony Messenger Press, 1995), p. 12.

Chapter 8 The Art of Growing in Greater Love of Yourself

[1] Santayana, George, *The Life of Reason, I, Reason and Common Sense*, (Charles Scribner's Sons, 1905).

[2] Augustine, Saint, Bishop of Hippo, *The Confessions of St. Augustine*, (Sanage Publishing House 2021), Book 10, Sections 28 & 39: PL 32, 795.

[3] Frankl, Victor, *Man's Search for Meaning*, (Beacon Press, 2006).

[4] All of the actions listed here for how to take responsibility for your money are explained in detail in *Dave Ramsey's Complete Guide to Money*, by **Dave Ramsey**, (Lampo Press, Brentwood, TN, 2012). If you're looking for practical information to answer all your "How?" "What?" and "Why?" questions about money, this book is for you. It covers the A to Z of Dave's money teaching, including how

to budget, save, dump debt and invest. You'll also learn all about insurance, mortgage options, marketing, bargain hunting and the most important element of all--giving. This is the handbook of Financial Peace University.

Chapter 9   Loving Your Enemies

[1] "Nelson Mandela transformed himself and then his nation," (L.A. Times Archives, Dec. 6, 2013).

Chapter 10   The Art of Growing in Greater Love of Others

[1] **Mary Kay Ash**, *The Mary Kay Way, Timeless Principles from America's Greatest Woman Entrepreneur*, (John Wiley and Sons, Inc., Hoboken, New Jersey, 2008), p. 39.

[2] **Martin B. Copenhaver**, *Jesus is the Question, The 307 Questions Jesus Asked and the 3 He Answered*, (Abingdon Press, Nashville, Tennessee, 2014), p. xxiii.

Bibliography

Alphonso, Herbert. *Discovering Your Personal Vocation: The Search for Meaning through the Spiritual Exercises.* Mahweh, New Jersey: Paulist Press, 2001.

Ash, Mary Kay. *Timeless Principles from America's Greatest Woman Entrepreneur.* Hoboken, New Jersey: John Wiley and Sons, Inc. 2003.

Augustine, Saint, Bishop of Hippo. *The Confessions of St. Augustine.* Mumbai, Maharashtra, Sanage Publishing House 2021. Book 10, Sections 28 & 39: PL 32,795.

Barry, W. A. *Paying Attention to God: Discernment in Prayer.* Notre Dame, Ind.: Ave Maria Press, 1990.

Bauerschmidt, Frederick. *Why Mystics Matter Now.* Notre Dame, IN, Sorin Books, 2003.

Brother Lawrence of the Resurrection. Trans. John J. Delaney, *The Practice of the Presence of God.* New York: Image Books, 1977.

> The spirit of a Carmelite kitchen brother of the seventeenth century who lived his life as prayer, emanates from the pages of this short book. Ultimately, discernment depends on a close personal relationship with God; this book helps lay the groundwork for that relationship to develop.

Carus, Paul (Editor). *Sayings of Buddha*. Peter Pauper Press, 1957.

Copenhaver, Martin B. Jesus is the Question, *The 307 Questions Jesus Asked and the 3 He Answered*. Nashville, Tennessee: Abingdon Press, 2014.

Farrington, Debra K. *Hearing with the Heart, A Gentle Guide to Discerning God's Will for Your Life*. San Francisco: Jossey-Boss, 2003.

Farrington, Debra K. *Learning to Hear with the Heart, Meditations for Discerning God's Will*. San Francisco: Jossey-Boss, 2003.

Frankl, Victor. *Man's Search for Meaning*. Boston, Mass., Beacon Press, 2014.

Fromm, Erich. *The Art of Loving*. New York, Hagerstown, San Francisco, London: Harper and Row, 1974.

Futrell, John Carroll. *Ignatian Discernment*, Vol. 2, no. 2 of *Studies in the Spirituality of Jesuits*. St. Louis: American Assistancy Seminar on Jesuit Spirituality, 1969.

> A primer for understanding the language and meaning of the "Rules for the Discernment of Spirits" section of *The Spiritual Exercises of St. Ignatius*. The paper strives to teach how to apply Ignatian concepts of discernment to the situations of everyday life.

Ignatius of Loyola. *The Spiritual Exercises of Ignatius of Loyola*. A Translation and Commentary by George E. Ganss, S.J. Chicago: Loyola Press, 1992.

Ignatius of Loyola. *Spiritual Exercises and Selected Works*, ed. George E. Ganss. Mahwah, New Jersey: Paulist Press, 1991.

Lewis, C.S. *The Four Loves*. San Diego, New York, London. Harcourt Brace Jovanovich, 1960.

Lewis, C.S. *The Great Divorce*. New York, Harper Collins, 2015.

Lonsdale, David. *Eyes to See, Ears to Hear—An Introduction to Ignatian Spirituality*. Maryknoll, New York, Orbis Books, 2000.

Lubich, Chiara. *The Art of Loving*. Hyde Park, New York: New City Press, 2010.

Lubich, Chiara. *Essential Writings*. Hyde Park, New York: New City Press, 2007.

Merton, Thomas. *Thoughts in Solitude*. New York: Farrar, Straus and Giroux, by The Abbey of Our Lady of Gethsemani, 1958.

Merton, Thomas. *New Seeds of Contemplation*. New York: New Directions, 1972.

> One of Merton's most widely read works, this book offers profound reflections on humility, obedience, detachment, personal identity and the contemplative experience.

Pysalski, Rev. Leo C.SS.R., *The Holy Will of God, Source of Peace and Happiness*. Rockford, Illinois: Tan Books and Publishers, Inc., 1947.

Ramsey, Dave. *Dave Ramsey's Complete Guide to Money*. Brentwood, TN, Lampo Press, 2011.

Rosenberg, PhD, Marshall. *Nonviolent Communication—A Language of Life.* Encinitas, CA, Puddle Dancer Press, 2015.

This seminal book offers dynamic communication techniques that can transform potential conflicts into peaceful dialogue. It also teaches a way of communicating that helps to avoid triggering a defensive reaction.

Russell, Bertrand. *Power: A New Social Analysis*, 1938, Chapter One. (Unwin Books, 1983).

Sanford, John. *Dreams: God's Forgotten Language.* San Francisco: Harper & Row, 1968, 1989.

Tada, Joni Eareckson. *Finding God in Hidden Places.* Eugene, Oregon, Harvest House Publishers, 1999.

Teresa of Calcutta, Saint. *In the Heart of the World: Thoughts, Stories and Prayers*, New World Library, 1997.

Thomas, Andrew. "How Training These Service Dogs Helps Veterans Heal." *The Epoch Times*, 9-15 Sept., 2020.

Whitman, Walt. *Songs of Myself, 48, Leaves of Grass:Unabridged Deathbed Edition with 400 Poems.* Seawolf Press, 2023.

ABOUT THE AUTHOR

"A Life of Four Paths"

Each time I embarked on a new path, I always jumped in with both feet as if that way held the key to finding truth, meaning and love. That approach not only helped me gain a deep knowledge about each path, but also to have a felt experience of it as well.

Path #1: <u>The Seminary & Teaching Path:</u> After graduating from college and falling short of my childhood dream of becoming a professional baseball player, my search for truth and love began in the seminary where I trained for seven years to become a Jesuit priest. After completing my theological studies at the Graduate Theological Union in Berkeley, California, I left the Jesuits short of ordination and gave Intensive Journal workshops developed by Dr. Ira Progoff helping people gain a deeper understanding of themselves and their relationships through the power of journal writing. Shortly thereafter, I completed an M.A. in Religious Education and taught, counseled, coached and gave 20 retreats on the high school level.

Path #2: <u>The Eastern Path:</u> As a practitioner of the Eastern Path that included elements of the Buddhist and Hindu traditions, I spent the next seven years studying, engaging spiritual practices and meditating in hopes of one day becoming enlightened. After compiling a five volume compendium of the main tenets and practices of the Eastern Path, I left this way and engaged in a rigorous study of the different schools of psychology and personality typologies.

Path #3: <u>The New Thought/Self-Help Path:</u> My next path took the form of a five-year study, practice and teaching of "New Thought" and "Self-Help" ideologies, which incorporated much of the world view and teachings of the East. While enjoying "the good life" that financial independence afforded me, I was sailing along serving my two adopted daughters from China when I lost everything in a bad investment.

Path #4: <u>The Jesus Path:</u> Becoming a delivery driver to make ends meet, it was not until three years later that I was finally open to hear the truth about how I had been avoiding relationship with myself, others and God. With God still at a distance and a basement level of self-love and love of others in my relationship bag, I felt impelled to discover love's true meaning and how to go about loving for real.

It was within the Gospels that I unearthed the practice of love which Jesus practiced and encouraged everyone to do the same. It was this simple yet profound practice that opened the door to achieving peace of heart and happiness that I, and now many others, had never known before.

Index

Introduction

ONE   **What Is the Practice of Love?**

The practice of love in the lives of Pat, Gram and Janie, 5

Examples of the practice of love in action, 10

The three main actions involved when engaging the practice of love with others, 13

More examples of the practice of love in action, 13

The practice of love is also about being and basking in the presence of those we love, including our animals, 16

TWO   **Why Engage the Practice of Love?**

Three Reasons:

1. Love is eternal. In contrast, everything else is temporary, 19
2. It makes us most happy, 21
3. It enhances the quality of all our relationships, 24

THREE   **The Practice of Love and the Jesus Path**

        Jesus engaged the practice of love with others, 27

        Jesus engaged the practice of love with his Father, 29

        Jesus urged everyone to engage the practice of love, 32

        Summary, 34

FOUR   **What Stands in the Way of Hearing the Truth?**

        The rich man's obstacle, 38

        Part one of our lives is spent building our identity and reputation, 40

- ~ We've worked hard for our image and reputation and don't want to lose it, 41
- ~ Why do we hold on so tightly to our identity and reputation?, 42

        How do we go about forming our identity and reputation?, 43

        Some identities I've created or assumed over the course of my life, 45

        The identities of Moses in the form of negative beliefs, 48

        What negative beliefs do you have that are keeping you stuck?, 49

How identifying with fear, sorrow or anger can close the door to truth, 51

Summary, 52

FIVE **The Ultimate Choice: Obey God or Chart Your Own Course**

Adam and Eve's choice to disobey God, 53

Our culture wholeheartedly supports charting your own course by relying on self-effort, 54

The Jesus Path also advocates taking action, but action issuing forth from one's personal relationship with Jesus, 56

Four fishermen's choice to follow Jesus, 57

God gives us the freedom to choose however we want to be, 59

SIX **The Art of Growing in Greater Love of God**

One primary way of growing in greater love of God is to consistently engage the practice of love, 63

Conscience is the link between ourselves and God, 64

Few people recognize that discernment or doing our best to listen to and follow God speaking through our conscience, lies at the heart of Christian spirituality, 66

A consideration of the six most common avenues through which the Spirit of truth speaks:

1. People, 67

    ~ The characteristics to look for in choosing a spiritual confidante, 68

2. Our body, 68

3. Our gut or intuition, 70

4. Common sense, conventional wisdom and important facts and information, 71

5. Sacred Scripture and Church teaching, 73

6. The experiences and details of everyday life, 75

Three Steps to making a thorough, God-guided decision, 76

How to tell when God is communicating versus your own ego or other influences, 78

If our intention is to follow God and do what is right, we will eventually get it right, 80

Summary, 82

SEVEN   **Seven Ways to Help Deepen Your Love of God**

1. Love God by loving your neighbor, 83

2. Contemplate the life of Jesus using your imagination, 85

3. Meditate on the life, death and resurrection of Jesus in a personal way by watching The Chosen, The Passion of Christ and its sequel, The Passion of Christ: Resurrection, 87

4. Have written dialogues with God, 88

5. Be grateful for everyday blessings, 89

6. Be aware of God's presence in the ordinary and pleasurable activities of life and converse with him throughout the day, 91

7. Find God's peace by praying with millions on hallow.com, the #1 prayer app in the world, 94

EIGHT   **The Art of Growing in Greater Love of Yourself**

How we develop a level of self-love that is lower than we'd like, 95

Why is it essential to grow in genuine self-love?, 96

Six ways to help you grow in genuine self-love:

1. Embrace your past and learn from it rather than accept it as a life-sentence, 98

2. Consistently engage the practice of love, 100

3. Let go of trying to please or control others to make you feel okay, 100

4. See yourself as God sees you, 104

5. Discover what gives ultimate meaning and purpose to your life, 108

    Why did some give up hope and die in the concentration camp at Auschwitz? 109

    Why did others survive? 110

    The difference between a man-centered and God-centered purpose, 111

6. Identify positive changes you want to make in the following six key areas of life and then begin taking responsibility for them one action at a time: 112

    a. Body, 113

    b. Emotions, 114

    c. Relationships, 115

    d. What you focus on, 116

    e. Money, 118

    f. Work, 119

Summary, 120

NINE   **Loving Your Enemies**

Loving your enemies is not easy and does not happen overnight, 125

Identifying your enemies, 127

How to go about loving your enemies:

1. Ask God to help you to even consider forgiving your enemies, 128
2. Forgive, but not too quickly. Release your feelings first, 129
3. Pray, bless and do good to those who hate, curse or mistreat you, 130
4. Engage the practice of love with them, 130
5. Walk a mile in their shoes, 131
6. See them through God's eyes, 133

Summary, 133

TEN   **The Art of Growing in Greater Love of Others**

The principle way of growing in love of others is to take on the practice of love, 137

A lack of engaged listening has reached epidemic proportions, 137

No one is born with the ability to listen skillfully—it must be learned, 139

Love in Action ~ Five steps to becoming the best listener and communicator you can be:

1. Become aware of your listening blocks, 142

2. Practice these tips to become a better listener, 144

3. Pay attention to non-verbal messages, 149

4. Switch from sending "You" messages to "I" messages, 153

    ~ "You" Messages Assessment, 154

    ~ What are "I" statements and how can they be used to elicit a positive change in behavior?, 155

5. Practice these tips to become a better communicator, 158

ELEVEN   A Side-By-Side Comparison of When *You Are* and *Are Not* Engaging the Practice of Love with Others

When you are not engaging the practice of love. . ., 170

When you are engaging the practice of love. . ., 170

TWELVE   Moving Forward: Cultivating the Art of Growing in Greater Love of Yourself, Others and God

The key to growing in greater love, 173

Three relationships are strengthened whenever you engage the practice of love, 174

Genuine love involves a commitment to love on purpose, 176

It's all about relationship, 177

Dear Reader,

Thank you for reading my book. I look forward to meeting you someday whether at a retreat, workshop, speaking engagement, phone consult or reaching out via email. For more information, please visit my website at davebeswick.net.

Dave

Made in the USA
Middletown, DE
11 February 2025